See!
I will not
forget you . . .
I have carved

you
on the palm
of my hand.

Isaiah 49:15

TO GOD BE THE GLORY

+++++++

SEE! I WILL NOT FORGET YOU ...
I HAVE CARVED YOU ON THE
PALM OF MY HAND

ISAIAH 49:16

+++++++

2012

SISTER ALVINA MILLER
DOMINCAN SISTERS OF PEACE
3600 Broadway
Great Bend, Kansas 67530

Table of Contents

Reflections from Sister Irene Hartman OP

When I was a student in the eighth grade, I had probably heard about Catherine the Great of Russia under whose tyrannical regime many citizens immigrated to the United States. They came in search of religious freedom and escape from the compulsory military service. But all that bit of history meant little of me, safe here in the United States, never a victim of governmental tyranny.

But when I entered the convent, I lived side by side with some members whose parents were part of that great exodus, people who had made their homes especially in Ellis County, Kansas. I heard bits and pieces of the families' struggles with poverty, customs, and language, but who were ever possessed with an eagerness to become part of the American scene by building churches, homes, and families, while seeking profitable employment.

I took even a closer look at the tragedy of the tyrannical rule in Russia when Sister Alvina Miller asked me to write her life story. Though I never met her mother Alvina Miller, an immigrant, nor her father Adam Miller, son of an immigrant, I feel that I know them both from their faith-based stories which I studied.

My journey with the Adam and Alvina Miller family has deepened my appreciation of this valiant family. I say "Thank you" to Sister Alvina for giving me this opportunity to record a moving and exciting adventure of faith. This is Sister Alvina's story, in which it becomes clear that her name is indeed carved in the palm of God's hand, the God who has seen her through the high and low times of a life well lived on the plains of Kansas, USA.

Prologue

"If we would always wait until life was given to us as gift, as opposed to taking it as if by right, seizing it, we would never break a single commandment; moreover we would have in our lives the first and most important virtue of all, the sense that all is gift, that nothing is owed us by right."

Walking with God "in the valleys" and "on the mountain tops"

"in the valleys"

Fully aware that my name is carved in God's palm, I have walked in God's grand creation with love and courage at these times in my ninety-four years:

- When I left home and missed so much the little two-year-old brother for whom we had waited for twelve years
- When I gave up teaching after thirty-two years with God's little ones
- When I said my last goodbye to my precious Papa when he was eighty-one
- When I concluded eleven energizing years in pastoral ministry
- When I live at a time of scarcity of priests and recognize that women are not allowed to fill in that gap

"on the mountain tops"

My "on the mountain top" days have been occasions when gratitude has guided my every step on a path marked with these wonderful gifts from an ever-attentive God:

- The gift of becoming a member of the Catholic Church through Baptism
- Learning to be at home in all manner of darkness
- The precious gift of a desire and the leisure for contemplative prayer
- The call and response to be a Dominican Sister of Peace
- The honor of preparing many little children for First Communion
- The spirit of poverty whereby I call nothing my own but have necessary things for my use
- For Sister Aloysia who encouraged Sisters to attain Masters degrees
- The privilege of making a thirty-day retreat in Sedalia, Colorado
- For a marvelous over-seas trip to five countries
- The privilege of serving as a parish minister
- For the blessing of clear vision at ninety-four
- Spiritual companionship with Father Donald Heim and Sister Renee Dreiling
- For good health and zest for life
- For a great capacity to listen, to learn, to be curious, to be open-minded
- For being a number five on the Enneagram, striving to be sympathetic, gentle, and patient

For all these blessings "in valleys" and "on mountain tops," I say "Thanks, God!"

I am an Aquarius   My birthday is February 17, 1918

You are the enthusiastic inventor of the world. Able to see the world as it should be or could be rather than as it is, you have the capacity to set things in motion.

Detached and impersonally friendly to all, you have many acquaintances. You are a dedicated humanitarian and very talented. You function well in groups and organizations as long as you can maintain your independence. Freedom is extremely important to you and you need to be able to do your own work your own way.

You are often politically involved as you see certain ordinary aspects of our culture and society as truly strange. Needing to be different, some aspect of your personality will be seen as eccentric by others.

Foreword

"Every person's life is God's work of art, an expression of one of God's creative love, His goodness, His compassion."

There are several reasons why I wanted to put my life story into print. During the years when I worked in St. John Parish in Hoisington, I had some leisure time which I devoted to writing my life story. I had the use of a word processor and began to record the memories of a lifetime.

I had always been interested in the history of the Russian German immigrants who settled in Ellis County, because I came from that line of settlers. My great grandparents and my paternal grandfather were born in Graf, Russia. My maternal grandfather, grandmother, and Mama were also born in Russia. I wrote my story because I want my generation and those following me to gratefully remember that we are the descendants of brave immigrants.

Sister Suzanne Noffke OP suggests that doing history is in fact "sacramental remembrance." She believes and I agree that the stories from the past can "form and transform us now, to shape our present into the future." She calls writing history a sacred ministry.

I have included in my life story many facts from my personal history but also my spiritual journey through the years. I firmly believe that any relationship with God has to be authentic, and I have tried to show that my aim has always been to develop an intimate relationship with God. Especially in writing my spiritual journey, I have taken a risk in showing my readers a tiny glimpse of how I see my good God.

"All pilgrims need to know that the longer one journeys toward Christ, the more likely the path will take a turn through dark places, and that finding ourselves in the dark is a sign of favor, not failure, and a sign of closeness. Sometimes I cannot see Christ, or much of anything, because my face is buried in His chest." (Susan R. Pitchford)

ACKNOWLEDGEMENTS

I would like to thank Sister Irene Hartman for her encouragement and for writing my life story. She spent many hours in searching my large collection of stories and pictures in my life and has very ably put it together in book form. I am truly grateful.

Also, I am grateful to Sister Cecilia Ann Stremel for printing the quote on the cover of this book. Sister has used her wonderful gift of calligraphy to make it look beautiful.

It tells very much of what my life has been about. Jesus has been my lover all these wonderful years. He has played with me, sighed with me, lamented with me, wept with me and laughed with me, and above all helped me live my life. Just sitting with Jesus and listening has been my greatest gift. You know, I cannot know Jesus in this life but I can always LOVE HIM.

Four Generations in the Family of Sister Alvina Miller

Sister Alvina Miller   born Feb. 17, 1918   died

Mama...Alvina Schuvie
b. Dec. 28, 1895   d. Feb. 16, 1989

Mama's parents
Anthony Schuvie   **Katherine Seib Schuvie**
b. Feb. 3, 1874   b. May 10, 1873
d. Nov. 8, 1958   d. June 11, 1941

Mama's grandparents
Fred Seib   **Julia Seib Schuvie**

Sister Alvina Miller   born Feb. 17, 1918   died

Papa...Adam Miller
b. April 19, 1890   d. June 25, 1971

Papa's parents
Jacob Miller Jr.   **Ottilia Schueler Miller**
b. July 14, 1850   b. Oct. 15, 1858
d. May 7, 1924   d. June 23, 1908

Papa's grandparents
Jacob Mueller Sr.   **Margaret Dorzweiler Mueller**
b. May 10, 1825   b. May 1, 1825
d. Feb. 14, 1905   d. July 8, 1909

**Marriage of Alvina Schuvie and Adam Miller
St. Catherine Church, Catherine, Kansas
Sept. 14, 1915**

The Family of Adam and Alvina Schuvie Miller

Adam Miller   born April 19, 1890   died June 25, 1971 (81)
Alvina Schuvie Miller born Dec. 28, 1895   died Feb. 16, 1989 (94)
> Married at St. Catherine Church, Catherine, Kansas on Sept. 14, 1915

Children, Grandchildren and Great Grandchildren

Amelia   b. Oct. 31, 1916   d. Dec. 8, 1999 (83)
> Married Edmund Meis on Sept. 30, 1935
>   b. June 25, 1915   d. Nov. 29, 2008 (93)

> Imelda (Sister Ronald CSA) b. Aug. 12, 1936 d. Feb. 2, 2013 (77)
> Ernest   b. Dec. 2, 1938   d. Apr. 13, 2010 (72)
> Robert   b. Jan. 21, 1940   d. June 9, 2006   (66)
> Paul   b. Feb. 11, 1942   d.
> Herbert   b. June 24, 1945   d. Apr. 24, 1994 (49)
> Harold   b. Nov. 7, 1947   d. Apr. 20, 2013 (65)

Emertina   b. Feb. 17, 1918   d.
> Professed as Sister Alvina   Aug. 20, 1935

Arthur   b. July 24, 1930   d. Nov. 14, 2011 (81)
> Married Maria Magiera Feb. 4, 1955
>   b. Feb. 2, 1928   d.

Cecil   b. Jan. 10, 1937   d.
> Married Gloria Luea on Aug. 4, 1956
>   b. Mar. 23, 1935   d.

Cecil's children on next page

Jeff   b. Feb. 14, 1959   d.
    Married Dottie Henning March 21, 1987
       Dottie Henning b. June 24, 1962   d.
         Adam   b. May 12, 1991   d.
         Jessica   b. Oct. 10, 1994   d.   .

Jenifer   b. June 13, 1962   d.
    Married Dwight Jones March 24, 2001
       Dwight Jones b. Aug. 11, 1962   d.
         Landry   b. Jan. 24, 2003   d.

Jackie   b. June 1, 1965   d.
    Married Shaun Price June 7, 1996
       Shaun Price b. June 28, 1962   d.
    Adopted four children:
       Stratton   b. Apr. 25, 1993   d.
       Cory   b. Apr. 2, 2003   d.
       Jada   b. Oct. 8, 2003   d.
       Ariel   b. May 23, 2006   d.

Leota Miller Howard, daughter of John and Rose Miller, double first cousin, became part of the Adam Miller family when Leota's mother died when she was about 2 year old. She was not legally adopted but was brought up as a member of the family.
Leota Miller Howard   b. Aug. 23, 1921   d. July 23, 2008

****

SIBLINGS in the family:

1. Amelia was born Oct.31, 1916 and died December 8, 1999.
   She married Edmund Meis Sept. 30, 1935.
   Edmund was born June 25, 1915. He died Nov. 29, 2008
   Children of Amelia and Edmund:
   Sister Ronald CSA, Ernest, Paul, Robert, Hal, Herbert.

2. Emertina Odilia was born February 17, 1918.
   As Sister Alvina, she was invested with the Dominican habit
   March 27, 1933.
   She made profession as a Dominican Sister in Great Bend
   August 20, 1935.

3. Arthur was born July 24, 1930 and died Nov. 14, 2011.
   He married Maria Magiera from Germany February 4, 1955.

4. Cecil Miller was born January 10, 1937.
   He married Gloria Luea August 4, 1956.
   Children of Cecil and Gloria:
   Jeff married Dottie Henning and had two children:
   Adam and Jessica.
   Jenifer married Dwight Jones and had one child, Landry.
   Jackie married Shaun Price and adopted four children.

Leota Miller was born August 23, 1921, and died July 23,
   1992. She became part of the Miller family after the death
   of her mother when Leota was about two years old. She
   was not legally adopted but was brought up as a member
   of the Adam and Alvina Miller family.

Poem "Heaven's Very Special Child," for the fifth son of Amelia and Edmund Meis, Herbert, who was developmentally challenged:

From the Memorial Card of Herbert Meis   b. June 2, 1945
                                          d. Apr. 24, 1994

A meeting was held quite far from earth,
It's time again for another birth,
Said the angels to the Lord above
This special child will need much love.
His progress may seem very slow,
Accomplishments he may not show,
And he'll require extra care
From the folks he meets down there.
He may not run, or laugh, or play,
His thoughts may seem quite far away,
In many ways he won't adapt
And he'll be known as handicapped.
So let's be careful where he's sent,
We want his life to be content.
Please, Lord, find the parents who
Will do this special job for you.
They will not realize right away,
The leading role they're asked to play.
But with this child sent from above,
Comes stronger faith and wider love.
Soon they'll know the privilege given
In caring for this gift from heaven,
This special charge, so meek and mild,
Is heaven's very special child.

No. ....

UNITED STATES OF AMERICA

Department of Commerce and Labor
BUREAU OF IMMIGRATION AND NATURALIZATION
DIVISION OF NATURALIZATION

PETITION FOR NATURALIZATION

District Court of *Ellis Co. Kans.*

In the matter of the petition of Jacob Miller (was Mueller) *to be admitted a citizen of the United States of America.*

To the District *Court of* Ellis Co. Kans.

The petition of Jacob Miller *respectfully shows:*

First. My full name is Jacob Miller

Second. My place of residence is number _____ street, city of Catharine Kansas State Territory of Kansas

Third. My occupation is Farmer

Fourth. I was born on the 14th day of July, anno Domini 1860, at Catharine, Russia

Fifth. I emigrated to the United States from Hamburg, Germany, on or about the 3rd day of July anno Domini 1878, and arrived at the port of New York, in the United States, on the vessel _____

Sixth. I declared my intention to become a citizen of the United States on the 27th day of July anno Domini 1877 at Hays City, court of District of Ellis Co. Kans.

Seventh. I am married. My wife is dead. Ottie Von Schmidt was born in Catharine, Russia and now resides at _____ and the name, date and place of birth, and place of residence of each of said children is as follows: _____

Eighth. I am not a disbeliever in or opposed to organized government or a member of or affiliated with any organization or body of persons teaching disbelief in organized government. I am not a polygamist nor a believer in the practice of polygamy. I am attached to the principles of the Constitution of the United States, and it is my intention to become a citizen of the United States and to renounce absolutely and forever all allegiance and fidelity to any foreign prince, potentate, state, or sovereignty, and particularly to Nicholas, 2nd, Emperor of Prussia of which at this time I am a subject, and it is my intention to reside permanently in the United States.

Ninth. I am able to speak the English language. I can read and write English. I can write and read German.

Tenth. I have resided continuously in the United States of America for a term of five years at least immediately preceding the date of this petition, to wit, since the 21 day of July, anno Domini 1878, and in the State of Kansas for one year at least next preceding the date of this petition, to wit, since the 21 day of July anno Domini 1878.

Eleventh. I have not heretofore made petition for citizenship to any court. _____

Dated March 5th 1910

Jacob Miller

State of Kansas
County of Ellis

Jacob Miller, being duly sworn, deposes and says that he is the petitioner in the above-entitled proceeding; that he has read the foregoing petition and knows the contents thereof; that the same is true of his own knowledge, except as to matters therein stated to be alleged upon information and belief, and that as to those matters he believes it to be true.

Subscribed and sworn to before me this 5th day of March anno Domini 1910
[SEAL.] N. M. Stanton, Clerk

Declaration of Intention and Certificate of Landing from Department of Commerce and Labor filed this 5th day of March 1910
N. M. Stanton, Clerk

AFFIDAVIT OF WITNESSES

In the matter of the petition of Jacob Miller *to be admitted a citizen of the United States of America*

State of Kansas
County of Ellis

Geo. H. Brown occupation Sheriff of Deeds residing at Hays, Kansas and W. Schuler, Jr. occupation Register of Deeds residing at _____

each being severally, duly, and respectively sworn, deposes and says that he is a citizen of the United States of America; that he has personally known Jacob Miller, the petitioner above mentioned, to be a resident of the United States for a period of at least five years continuously immediately preceding the date of filing his petition, and of the State in which the above-entitled application is made for a period of one year immediately preceding the date of filing his petition; and that he has personal knowledge that the said petitioner is a person of good moral character, attached to the principles of the Constitution of the United States, and that he is in every way qualified, in his opinion, to be admitted a citizen of the United States.

Geo. H. Brown
A. Schuler, Jr.

[SEAL.] Subscribed and sworn to before me this 5 day of March anno Domini 1910
N. M. Stanton, Clerk

Jacob Mueller Miller—Petition for Naturalization

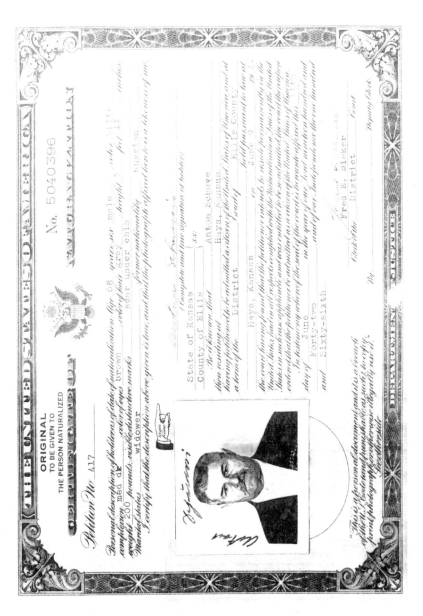

THE UNITED STATES OF AMERICA

No. 5040396

ORIGINAL
TO BE GIVEN TO
THE PERSON NATURALIZED

Petition No. 417

Personal description of holder as of date of naturalization: Age 68 years; sex male
complexion med dk color of eyes brown color of hair white height 5 feet 11 inches
weight 200 pounds; visible distinctive marks scar under chin
Marital status widower former nationality Russian
I certify that the description above given is true, and that the photograph affixed hereto is a likeness of me.

Anton Schuve

State of Kansas   }
County of Ellis   } ss:

Be it known that Anton Schuve
then residing at Hays, Kansas
having petitioned to be admitted a citizen of the United States of America and
a term of the District Court of Ellis County
held pursuant to law at
Hays, Kansas on June 9 19
the court having found that the petitioner intends to reside permanently in the
United States (when so required by the Naturalization Laws of the United
States) in such cases applicable, and was entitled to be admitted to citizenship,
ordered that the petitioner be admitted as a citizen of the United States of America
In testimony whereof the seal of the court is hereunto affixed this
day of June in the year of our Lord nineteen hundred and
Forty-two and of our Independence the one hundred and
Sixty-sixth

Fred E. Bieker
Clerk of the District Court

By Deputy Clerk

"This is a personal document and to convert
of this U.S. Code any other photostat or other
furnish photocopy of copies there are illegally used."

Anthony and Katherine Sieb Schuvie
Rose, Frank, Margaret and Alvine

Fred and Julia Seib, Mother's grandparents

Passport of Anton Schuvie from Russia

23

Immigrants Head for the Ocean Liners
as America Beckons

"How grateful we are to God who guided
our steps to this wonderful country
of the brave and the free,
and who has helped and guided the struggle
and vicissitudes of the pioneer days.
May his rich blessings rest
on the coming generations as it
rested on the PIONEERS."
(Christine Hokanson)

Catherine II of Russia was eager to have unsettled sections of land of her country populated, and began inviting colonists to Russia in late 1762. Her invitation called "manifest" assured the colonists freedom of religion, plus freedom from tax levies and land service for thirty years. Another benefit was freedom from military service for an indefinite period. Two Captains were sent to Frankfurt, Germany , to find settlers who wished to come to Russia. Eight thousand families, about twenty-five thousand persons, responded. These settlers were welcomed to Oranienbaum in Russia. By the spring of 1764, they settled southward toward Saratow near the Volga River. One hundred colonies were established on both sides of the river at a cost to the Russian government of $5,899,813 rubles. (At that time a ruble was about fifty cents in American money).

Much to the chagrin of the settlers, a military edict in June of 1871, limited the exemption from military service to ten years. For a few years, colonists were allowed to migrate without losing any of their property. Some scouts came to America, to Nebraska, to Arkansas, and even to Larned, Kansas. Only unfavorable reports surfaced, and immigration was forgotten for a short time.

 In January of 1874, a new edict subjected all colonists to military service for about six years. Catholics especially resented this new law because it prevented them for attending church services. Only members of the Greek Church could rise to an officer's rank.

After the first draft of soldiers was complete, an extraordinary exodus from Russia began. Many took passage on the steamship Ohio of the North German Lloyd on November 2, 1875, and after twenty –one days at sea landed in Baltimore on November 23, 1875. Many of this group lived in Topeka, Kansas, for a short while and then moved to Catherine, Kansas. Near Hays, land could be purchased for $5.00 an acre. These pioneers settled in small colonies in Liebenthal, Victoria, Munjor, Catherine, Pfiefer, and Schoenchen.

There were no Catholic Churches west of Salina at this time, but each settlement erected a cross about which the people gathered for devotions on Sundays and holydays. Priests from Salina ministered to the new immigrants. One of the first efforts of each little colony was to build a parish church, and each family also built a simple home.

On my father's side my great grandparents, grandparents, and parents were part of this exodus from Russia. They were known as Mueller's, and later were called Miller's who settled in the Catherine vicinity. It was there that my great grandfather homesteaded a large tract of land. He had paid $5.00 an acre and later he was able to give good-sized portions to each of his twelve children. This land stayed in our family until 1991 when it was sold to Ross Beach.

My mother's parents Anthony and Katherine Schuvie came from Graf, Russia, and settled on a farm south of Victoria. This couple arrived at Baltimore, MD, on May 19, 1908. Anthony's official papers when he made application for citizenship on April 25, 1914, declare he is no longer a subject of Nicholas II, emperor of all of Russia. Nor is he an anarchist nor a polygamist, and only wants to become a citizen of the United States of America, which he did June 11, 1941. That was 27 years before he became a citizen.

The following quotes about the Volga Germans are taken from the book entitled *Wir Wollen Deutsche Bleiben* (*We want to remain German*) by George J. Walters:

> "Some of the cherished virtues of the Germans are honesty, industry, thrift, temperance, piety, love of children, and respect for elders."

> "The peasant...from morning to night must work the fields over and over, whether the sun remains in the fields."

"Without knowing it, the Germans on the Volga remained pawns in the hands of a new royalty, emerging in the world scene."

"The Volga farmers, secure in their eighteenth century culture...a culture quite superior to that of their Russian neighbors...refused to step down and assimilate.

"The Germans left the Volga because 'there was no opportunity.' The farmers were becoming more impoverished by the hour. Although the population was growing, resources for that growth were shrinking and the price of wheat 'robbed them all.'"

"The inability of draftees to make their Easter obligation may be figured in the migration 'but it was also the absence of opportunity.'"

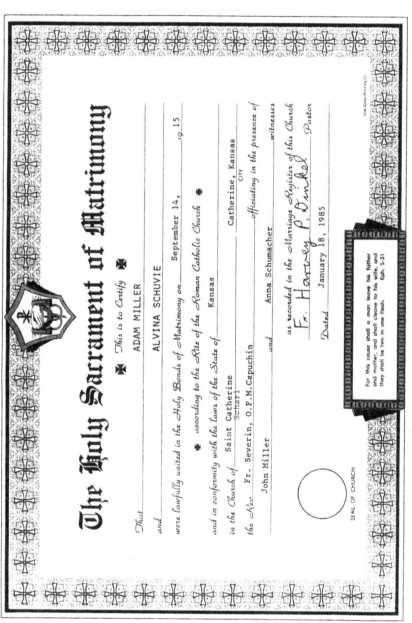

The Holy Sacrament of Matrimony

✠ This is to Certify ✠

That __ADAM MILLER__

and __ALVINA SCHUVIE__

were lawfully united in the Holy Bonds of Matrimony on __September 14,__ 19 __15__

✠ according to the Rite of the Roman Catholic Church ✠

and in conformity with the laws of the State of __Kansas__

in the Church of __Saint Catherine__ __Catherine, Kansas__

the Rev. __Fr. Severin, O.F.M.Capuchin__ __Scharl__ officiating in the presence of

__John Miller__ and __Anna Schumacher__ witnesses

as recorded in the Marriage Register of this Church

__Fr. Harvey P. Dinkel__ Pastor

Dated __January 18, 1985__

SEAL OF CHURCH

For this cause shall a man leave his father and mother, and shall cleave to his wife, and they shall be two in one flesh. Eph. 5-31

Certificate of Marriage—Adam and Alvina Miller

29

ADAM MILLER   Arthur   Sister Alvina   ALVINA SCHUVIE   1940

    AMELIA   Cecil   Leota

Adam and Alvina Miller Family

My parents' wedding picture, September 14, 1915

The Best of Teachers: Papa and Mama

Honor your father by word and deed, that
His blessing may come upon you. Sirach 3:8
Those who respect their father will have long
Life and those who honor their mother obey
The Lord.
Sirach 3:6

From all eternity I believe that God planned that I become a teacher of little children. As part of that plan, God blessed me with the best of teachers, my beloved Papa Adam and Mama Alvina Miller.

PAPA

Papa was born into a family of immigrants from the Volga River area in Russia: Jacob Mueller and Ottilia Schueler Mueller. This well-educated couple had migrated to Catherine, Kansas, America, in October of 1875, to escape the tyranny of the Russian government which required military service and which restricted religious observances.

Papa was born April 19, 1890, and grew up on his parents' family farm. When he became of a dating age, he dated Mama, arriving on horseback from his home near Catherine to her home near Victoria. They were married on September 14, 1915, in St. Catherine Church in Catherine , Kansas. After living with his parents for a short time, Papa and Mama moved to their own plot of formerly homestead land which had been given to the couple by Papa's father. My grandfather Jacob Mueller Jr. was an only child so from his father, my great grandfather, Jacob Mueller Sr., inherited all of great grandpa's homesteaded land. There my parents built the small home in which my siblings and I grew up.

I was the second daughter born into the Adam Miller family, and I was named Emertina Ottilia at my Baptism. Papa made great efforts to bring the doctor to our home when Mama went into labor, and again a second time when Mama began bleeding profusely. I will be always grateful to have such a wonderful father. I would describe him as one of my wisdom figures; from him I learned values to which I will always adhere.

When I think of Papa, I remember his great care for his family, his sense of humor, his strong belief in justice, his very tender heart, his gentle manner in dealing with difficulties in the family, his reverence for the name of God, his conservative spirit, his sharing of stories read in German, and his encouragement for my entering a religious community even though my leaving home brought many tears to his eyes. With his trust in me, I was able at age twelve to begin plowing the fields and managing three horses. Although there were times when Papa drank too much bourbon, I never felt that he ever abused Mama or the children God had entrusted to Papa's care.

Papa and Mama had a very beautiful married life; they were deeply in love with each other. They were happy together and they truly lived for each other. Their love was very evident; they even seemed to know each other's thoughts and feelings, and they had a deep respect for each other. Papa was not strong physically and I often felt sorry for him when he had to work so hard in the fields to provide for his family. He was a frugal man, a good provider, and often deprived himself of things he wanted so we could have what we needed. He would take a load of wheat to the elevator;

this was an all day job. He sold the wheat and we lived off the income until we needed to sell another load. Remembering the love we children had for sweets, Papa often came home with a bag of candy for us.

Papa was generous with his signs of love, but at times he seemed to be very stingy with his money. Sometimes we children had to beg often before Papa would finally give us what we thought we needed. Papa spent his money wisely and though he provided us with all we needed, he was not easily convinced we needed what we asked for.   Papa never bought anything unless he had the cash to pay for it.

It was evident that Papa had many friends and he enjoyed visiting with them on trips to town. Mama would do the grocery shopping while Papa visited. Then she would wait in the car until he was finished with his conversation with friends. She couldn't understand why he had so much to say to his friends.

There was never any doubt that Papa was a man of deep faith. He was always the leader for family prayer. Never neglected were morning prayer, meal prayer, evening prayer, and special prayer during Advent and Lent. During Lent, for night prayer we prayed the Rosary with outstretched arms in honor of the five wounds of Jesus. During October and May, we had special prayers in honor of Mary. During storms we lit candles for protection and sprinkled our home with holy water, while asking God for protection. This was a blessing because when lightening struck our house we were all safe except the house was damaged.

Another family custom I well remember was the visits with relatives and friends on New Years to wish them God's blessings. Our prayer was in German. The translation is: "I wish you a happy New Year, long life, health, peace and harmony, and after death eternal happiness."* We usually were given money, mostly nickels and dimes, or sometimes even a quarter. Our baptismal sponsors were the generous ones. I don't know if this was a custom adopted from Papa's or Mama's traditions.

Papa gave me encouragement when I was preparing to enter the Dominican convent in Great Bend. He realized how very much he would miss me, but he saw in my vocation his opportunity to give back to God, the daughter God had loaned to him. Papa was pleased that I chose to enter at Great Bend instead of Fond du Lac, Wisconsin, which was so far away. Meal time seemed a good time to discuss my vocational plans but these talks did not please my sister Amelia who was set on marriage. All through the next almost forty years, Papa continued to show his loving support for my choice of a religious vocation.

After a long and profitable life, Papa came to the end of his days in 1971. I was stationed in Sapulpa, Oklahoma, when I received the news of his approaching death. This was the year that our parish school was to be closed, hence the work at the end of the school year was multiplied. I was able to spend a couple of weeks with my parents before Papa died. My brother Arthur and his wife Mary, had been stationed in Italy for three years and they came home in June to be with my parents. Their time together was short. On June 24, 1971, Arthur and his wife Mary left for El Paso, Texas. The next morning my precious Papa was called HOME. Cecil and his family were living in Ohio at the time. Mama and I were alone to make all the funeral arrangements for the best possible of WIS-DOM FIGURE, MY PRECIOUS PAPA.

Papa, I thank you for your ever-present love and support for me.

The German for the New Years' wish:
   Ich wensche Euch ein glueckaeliges Heujahr,
   Langes Leben, Gesundeit, Friede und Einigkeit
   Nach dem Tode eie ewige Gluckseligkeit

Mama

Catherine the Great of Russia was eager to stimulate the coloniza-
tion of farmers from Germany and France to the area near the Volga River. She was searching for industrious farmers or models for
her own people whom she considered agriculturally inefficient and
backward. She extended promising rewards to the immigrants,
such as freedom from taxes for thirty years, a loan to pay for the
move of the newcomers, and freedom from military service. According to the French police, about 235 families who were German
-speaking farmers in France accepted the invitation. Among them
was my Mama's family, my Schuvie grandparents, Anton Schuvie,
and Katherine Seib Schuvie, from Alsace Lorraine, France. The family settled in Graf, Russia, where Mama, Albina Schuvie, was born
December 28, 1895.

Catherine's promises were not all kept, especially the freedom
from military service, and soon my grandparents began searching
for a new home in America. Because my Schuvie grandparents
were very poor, a kind family helped pay for the move. The family
consisted of the parents, and four children, Albina (Alvina), Frank,
Rose, and Margaret. After a fourteen-day voyage on a bug infested
ship, the family arrived in Baltimore, Maryland, on May 20, 1908,
and eventually settled on a farm south of Victoria, Kansas. The
newly immigrated family moved to a small house in Victoria.

To assist the family, Mama took jobs away from home, especially doing housework. This proved to be very difficult and tiring work, as well as time-consuming. There was no electricity; wood and coal had to be carried into the house for heating and cooking. Mama rose at 5:00 a.m. in order to begin the day's work. She milked the cows, separated the milk from the cream in a hand operated separator, prepared three meals a day, baked bread and pies, washed the clothes on a washboard, hung them on the line, and ironed them with an iron heated on the cook stove. Harvest time brought additional duties, such as taking meals to the workers in the field. The little she earned doing all this work was a great help for the family budget. By ten p.m., Mama literally fell into bed from exhaustion.

According to family records, Mama was able to attend early education for only one year because her meager income from work outside the home was so necessary for her struggling family. For many years she did not know how to read or write or do math. Later she did learn how to read, and could read the newspapers and her favorite prayer books. At eighty-three, she surprised the family by seeking this book from the library, LIFE AFTER LIFE. She wanted to know about people who had clinically died and then came back to life again. I believe Mama possessed a wisdom far beyond her years, and I profited by her work ethic and her dedication to the family she loved so much.

In 1915, Mama met Adam Miller, whose parents had migrated from Russia. Happy the day when Papa began courting Mama! He would come by horseback from Catherine to Victoria to visit her and in a short time there were marriage plans. My parents were married in St. Catherine Church in Catherine, Kansas, on September 14, 1915.

Mama gave birth to four children, two girls and later two boys. Amelia was born October 31, 1916, and died December 8, 1999. Emertina (Sister Alvina) was born February 17, 1918. Arthur was born July 24, 1930, and died November 14, 2011. Cecil was born January 10, 1937.

A very industrious woman, made so by the hardships that were part of her growing days, Mama was a very saving person. She never spent for things that she did not need; she managed with little. A creative person, she made her own laundry soap, wine and beer, cheese, and even starch; she canned fruits, vegetables, and meat. She considered cleanliness vital, even though as children, we liked to play in the dirt and mud. She was a generous person when the hungry appeared on her doorstep. Mama took in my cousin Leota whose mother died when the child was thirteen months old; Mama raised her as one of her own. Mama was a woman of faith, and passed on to us her passion for the good and the holy. After Papa's death, Mama drove herself to daily Mass whenever possible.

Mama possessed a bit of prejudice which was evident in her later days when she was living with my brother Arthur and sister-in-law Mary in Longview, Texas. There were times when they needed someone to stay with Mama when they were away from home. There was an African-American lady who would have been very willing to assist the family, but Mama resisted because the lady was black. As I remember there were times in years past when an African-American was not allowed to stay overnight in Hays. Perhaps this attitude still clung to Mama.

With a love for adventure and desire for travel, Mama would have enjoyed going to faraway places, but Papa did not have the same urge, so Mama was much a stay-at-home person. After Papa died on June 25, 1971, Mama did take trips to see my brother in El Paso and Longview, Texas. In her early eighties, she gave up driving; this pleased the family, for we feared for her safety. She had high blood pressure and there was the fear she might have a stroke while driving.

A very fond memory of Mama remains fresh in my mind. On one occasion, she told me she wanted to gift me with a car for my own use. I told her that I didn't need a personal car; when I needed one, I could use a community car. I told her that I did however have one special desire, namely to make a trip to the Holy Land. This very frugal Mama of mine, who as a young woman had toiled so many years from 5:00 a.m. until 10:00 p.m. in very difficult circumstances to assist her own parents, was now saying to me, "Of course, I will pay for your trip to the Holy Land!" She made my wish come true when in July of 1983, I experienced a marvelous trip to Cairo in Egypt, Amman in Jordan, Israel, Greece and Rome.

At eighty-seven, Mama was no longer able to live alone; she went to live with my brother Arthur and sister-in-law Mary in Longview, Texas. They tended to her needs until Mary had a mastectomy and was no longer able to give Mama the care she needed. Mama lived in a nursing home in Texas the last eleven months of her long life.

My precious Mama, a valiant and faith-filled woman, died on a Thursday morning February 16, 1989. Her body was shipped to Hays for burial. A memorial service was held in the Immaculate Heart of Mary Church, the parish to which my parents belonged when they retired from the farm. She was buried beside Papa in St. Joseph Cemetery in Hays.

Dearest Mama, I shall always be grateful to my God for the precious gift you were to me.

"Before you had a being,
  God loved you
Before your Father or Mother was born
  God loved you. Yes,
Even before the creation of the world
  God loved you...
GOD LOVED YOU FROM ETERNITY."

God took the strength of a mountain,
    The majesty of a tree,
  The warmth of a summer sun,
    The calm of a quiet sea,
  The generous soul of nature,
  The comforting arm of night,
    The wisdom of the ages,
  The power of the eagle's flight,
  The joy of a morning in spring,
  The faith of a mustard seed,
    The patience of eternity,
  The depth of a family need,
  Then God combined these qualities,
 When there was nothing more to add,
 He knew His masterpiece was complete,
        And so,
      He called it...Dad
                Author unknown

God bless my beloved parents.

Daughter Number Two Arrives in the Miller Home

"Holiness does not mean perfection.
The saints were always flawed,
limited, humans.
Holiness always makes its home
in humanity."
(James Martin S.J.)

My theme song for many of the wondrous years of my Spirit-filled life has been borrowed from my friend Isaiah 49:16. "See, I will not forget you. I have carved you on the palm of my hand." Some one shared with me this precious quote: "We want a God who tells us exactly which way to go and what to do next. Instead we find a God who meets us in the wilderness with the words, 'Don't be afraid. You are not lost. You are just a bit bewildered. If you want to know where the future leads, put your hand in mine and come and see.'"

On a cold blistery February day, February 17, 1918, I opened my bright eyes to look at God's great wide world. Mama had sent Papa to get the good doctor who made house calls and who delivered me safely even though I had the umbilical cord wound around my neck. After the doctor departed, Mama began having excessive bleeding and doctor returned to assist Mama. Prayer helped her to recover but sadly this setback made it impossible for Mama to conceive for another twelve years.

World War I was in progress when I was born; Woodrow Wilson was president. In 1917, the first airmail stamps were issued, and airmail delivery began in the United States. Little did I know the great events that were just beginning in my life: my call and response to the Maker of my being, going where I was called, doing what God had in mind for me, carrying the Good News of the Gospel to places near and far.

I was taken to St. Catherine Church in Catherine, Kansas, the next day for the blessed sacrament of Baptism, administered by Rev. Basil Heim, OFM Cap. My godparents were Uncle Frank and Aunt Rose Miller. Mama had chosen the name Emertina, a name she had found in a German book of saints. Emertina was said to have been the foster sister of St. Agnes, an early martyr. My name means "beloved by all." (Later I came to know that indeed God saw me as beloved and had me written on the palm of His hand at the moment of my Baptism).

My middle name Ottilia was from a saint in Alsace Lorraine at the end of the seventh century. The child was blind from birth and abandoned by her parents. Nuns educated the little girl. The bishop of Regensburg baptized her and she recovered her sight. (Can you see that already in the seventh century, I was connected with Regensburg, the city from which our Dominican ancestors came to establish the Order in the United States?) Eventually Ottilia's father received her back home and gave her property on which to establish a monastery. As the abbess of that community, she lived a prayerful and frugal life, giving attention lovingly to those in need. Her name means "daughter of light."

The name Helen was added to my name when I was confirmed as a postulant. How did that happen? When the bishop came to our parish the last time I was still at home, I was too young for the parish confirmation class. The day before my investing in 1933, during my visit with the bishop as was the customary thing to do, he noticed that I had not been confirmed. That afternoon he administered the sacrament and I was sealed with the seven gifts of the Holy Spirit. With the name Helen, I believed that I was indeed feeling the hand of God engraved on my life as Isaiah started to teach me.

Our Home and Life on the Family Farm

Our family farm was located seven miles north of Catherine or four miles east of Severin. Our mission church was located in Severin where we had Masses celebrated on Sundays and holydays.

I remember the noise of hammering as our home was being built when I was a little tot. Our home had four rooms: a kitchen, a dining and living room combined, two bedrooms, and half an unfinished basement. Our canned foods and the summer vegetables were stored in the basement. During the winter months, coal was also kept there. How I hated to clean the basement where I might encounter spiders and bugs! In later years a bathroom and two porches were added. There was no indoor plumbing; water had to be carried from the pump.

The buildings on our farm consisted of our house, a barn, a chicken house, a garage, a granary, and a wash house. The cooking was done on a coal-burning range. There was a reservoir which had to be kept filled; it was attached to the kitchen stove and it provided hot water for dish washing and cleaning. In summer we cooked and canned on a three-burner kerosene stove in the kitchen. In the wash house, there was a large kettle for doing laundry, and making sausage when we butchered. We cured and smoked the butchered meat and kept it in the barn loft during the winter months. Some of the meat was stored in lard in a large crock or canned in jars. We did not have electricity.

Some of my chores on the farm consisted of carrying water to fill the jug in the kitchen and to fill the reservoir. I shared with my siblings the task of bringing in corn cobs from the pig pen and cow chips from the pasture; these were used as kindling to start the fire. We fed and watered the chickens and the pigs, gathered eggs, brought the cows in from the pasture at milking time, milked cows, turned the separator to separate the milk from the cream, washed the separator, churned butter, made cheese, and tended the kerosene lamps. We installed carbide lights when I was about eleven. The new lights were a great improvement in our home, and later the installation of indoor plumbing was also a great blessing.

Harvest time on the farm meant much extra work, more farm help, meals and cold water carried to the workers, long hours in the fields, weary bones. Mother had the assistance of my sister Amelia and me to help prepare a ten a.m. lunch, and another meal in the afternoon, plus supper at the end of a hard day in the fields. When I was twelve, I was able to help Papa with the plowing. We had two plows and six horses. I found this to be very monotonous work, just sitting on the plow and riding up and down the rows all day long in the hot sun. Papa encouraged me to make straight rows and I tried to follow his example. To protect my fair skin, I wore overalls, a long sleeved shirt, and a bonnet. We truly cared for the earth and were grateful for the plot of land which Papa had inherited from his father, who had homesteaded it years ago. The land remained in our family until my brother Arthur and his wife Mary sold it to Ross Beach in 1991. The farm was described as Section 15, Township 12, and Range 17.

My childhood was not all work and no play. In the absence of TV and electronic games, in many ways we found times and places for fun. There were games of hide and go seek in the cane fields, I spy, and card games. We had fun catching fireflies in the summer evenings and wondered just how those little bugs could light up! Indoors there were jacks and a form of Chinese checkers. My sister and I also played with dolls and learned to walk on stilts. There were creative games we invented with cardboard and buttons.

Childhood Memories

I want to add a few precious memories from my childhood days. On one occasion when Mama started a fire in the cook stove in the kitchen, she dropped her wedding ring in the fire. Only later did she miss it and she went to search for the ring in the pile of ashes which had already been thrown outside. She was delighted to find it, but was saddened to find if had turned an ugly black. A good neighbor suggested that she use vinegar to restore to its original beauty. She was happy for the suggestion and after soaking it in vinegar, it was beautiful once again. My niece is proud to wear that beautiful ring today.

Mama was very protective of me as was evidenced on this occasion. Before we had a car, my family went to church in a buggy drawn by a horse. On one winter day, there was ice at the bottom of a little hill which we had to cross. We were frightened when the horse slipped and fell on the ice. From that day, Mama would always cover my eyes with her hand when we came to the descent from that little hill so that I would not be scared.

It was common in the summer to have electrical storms accompanied by rain, thunder, and lightning. Our house did not have lightning rods. On one occasion our house was struck by lightning which knocked off the chimney; inside the house the wallpaper in the dining room was torn loose, left the house by a north window, and then began to burn the wooden frames on the windows. Luckily rain came and put out the fire. The fear of lightning remains with me to this day and I refuse to be outdoors during an electrical storm.

My Search for the Stars

When I was ready to begin my early education, I found myself for my first three years under the tutelage of Katie Billinger in a two-room schoolhouse. What joy to begin opening the doors to the knowledge of reading, writing, and arithmetic! Sophie Hammerschmidt was my fourth grade teacher. Barbara Sander taught me in grades five and six, and Amelia Wasinger was my teacher in grades seven and eight. Our school year lasted only eight months, because most of the students were needed on their family farms in early spring. I loved school and seldom missed a day unless I was really sick; I had the record of having five years of perfect attendance.

Spelling was one of my favorite subjects and I came to be known as an excellent speller. On one occasion I misspelled the word 'separate' and the teacher seemed to delight in catching me with a misspelling. Never again will I misspell that word! Most of the students enjoyed the Friday afternoon matches, either in spelling or arithmetic. On the playground, the students all spoke their native language, namely German, but in the classroom there was English in all studies. I was proud that I grew up bi-lingual. The girls never wore uniforms, just plain dresses. We usually had only two school dresses so we could trade off on laundry days. Needless to say there was no indoor plumbing in the school building.

On cold blistery days with deep snow on the ground, Papa often walked with Amelia, Leota, and me to the school. There he would light the stove so the room would be warm when the teachers arrived. Many years the teachers boarded with our family and slept in the same bedroom with Amelia, Leota, and me. The three of us were crowded in one bed, and the two teachers in the other.

Perhaps this is a good time to introduce Leota Miller, my first cousin. When she was eighteen months old, her mother Rose died; my parents took her into our family and she became like our little sister. She had been born in 1921, and thus was a few years younger than Amelia and me. Although her father Uncle John remarried, she remained as part of our family. She joined the Great Bend Dominicans, becoming known as Sister Cyril, but she left during her novitiate days. She died in 1992.

PLACE OF BIRTH.   STATE OF KANSAS.   **26   3107**

County of _Ellis_   STATE BOARD OF HEALTH—DIVISION OF VITAL STATISTICS.

Township of _Catherine_   **STANDARD CERTIFICATE OF BIRTH.**

City of _Emmeram_ .... No.............. , street. Reg. No. _303_

Full Name of Child _Otelia   Miller_   { If child is not yet named, make
                                                       { supplemental report, as directed.

| Sex of Child _Female_ | Twin, triplet, or other? (To be answered only in event of plural births.) | Number in order of birth. | Legitimate. _yes_ | Date of birth _2_ _17_ 1918 (Month) (Day) (Year) |

Full Name.	**FATHER.** _Adam Miller_	Full Maiden Name.	**MOTHER.** _Alvina Schmae_
Residence.	_Catherine_	Residence.	_Catherine_
Color. _White_	Age at last birthday _27_ (Years.)	Color. _White_	Age at last birthday _22_ (Years.)
Birthplace. _Kansas_		Birthplace. _Kansas_	
Occupation. _Farmer_		Occupation. _Housewife_	

Number of children born to this mother, including present birth. _2_   Number of children of this mother now living _2_

CERTIFICATE OF ATTENDING PHYSICIAN OR MIDWIFE.

I hereby certify that I attended the birth of this child, who was _born alive_ at _11_ A. M.,
on the date above stated.   (Born alive or stillborn.)

* When there was no attending physician or
midwife, then the father, householder, etc.,
should make this return. A stillborn child is
one that neither breathes nor shows other evidence of life after birth.

(Signature) ....

                                               (Physician or midwife.)

Given name added from supplemental
report   191   Address ....

                         Filed _2/18_ 1918 _Ellen Hofmeister_
          Registrar.   Registrar.

Sister Alvina's birth certificate (Emertina Otilia)

Emertina as a baby (Sister Alvina)

St. Catherine's Church where I was baptized

Alvina   Adam Miller

Emertina ‑ Leota ‑ Amelia

The Miller family in front of their first car

Adam and Alvina Schuvie Miller

Papa on his 81st birthday, April 19, 1971

My Schuvie Grandparents

Remember
"I could have made human beings in such a way
that they had everything,
but I preferred to give different gifts to different people
so that they would all need each OTHER."
(God to Catherine of Siena)

Grandpa Anton Schuvie

A tall and headstrong Frenchman who had migrated from Alsace Lorraine to accept some great promises of Catherine the Great in Russia...this was my great Grandpa. Grandpa Anton Schuvie had been born on February 3,1874, in Graf, Russia, where his father expected to be exempt from military service and given home rule. But the Russian government did not keep its earlier-made promises and when military duty was on the horizon, Grandpa looked to America as a place of freedom. With his family of a wife and four children, including my Mama, Grandpa made plans to emigrate.

Friends of the family gave monetary assistance for the family to make the long trip to an unknown world. The first segment of the overland trip from Russia began before the Volga River froze for the winter season. Upon arriving in Germany, it was discovered that Mama had trachoma; this had to be eradicated before the family could proceed on their journey to America.

Mama, 12 years old, described the trip as a fourteen- day voyage on a dirty, bedbug-infested ship. In May of 1908, the family settled south of Victoria on a little farm. They had reached their "promised land" and prayed it would be better than the last "promised land" they had been invited to in Graf, Russia. There was much suffering from the extreme poverty of the family. Again, Mama being the oldest child, began working away from home to bring in a little cash to ward off starvation.

From the beginning of life in America, Grandpa was the authority figure and made all the decisions in the family. He sought to become a citizen in 1914, and presently I have a copy of the document , Declaration of Intent, wherein he declared he was not an anarchist, nor a polygamist, and wanted to make United States his permanent home. He became a citizen in 1942.

My personal feelings about Grandpa are mixed. There were times when I was actually afraid of him. I saw him as a man who showed that he was "the boss" at all times; no one could make perfect decisions like Grandpa could. I felt that he never favored my becoming a religious; maybe if I had chosen the married state, I would have been doing what Grandpa wanted. I have misgivings about how Grandpa viewed religious life; that conversation will have to wait until I meet him in heaven. At all times I received the complete affirmation of my parents in the choice of my state of life. Grandpa's approval was not vital to my life, even though I would have appreciated it.

In his later life, he suffered from extreme poverty, and my parents had to help him financially to pay the taxes on his little house on 14th Street in Hays. My parents did not have a surplus of money either and when they paid his taxes, it was with the agreement that my parents would get the deed to his house when he died. To save money, he chose to live in the basement and rent out the upper story. At his death on November 8, 1958, Papa and Mama had to pay his funeral expenses. Grandpa Schuvie is buried in the Hays Cemetery.

Grandma Katherine Seib Schuvie

Grandma Katherine Seib Schuvie was a very kind and gentle woman. She was born May 10th, 1873, and died June 11th, 1941. I have few memories of this great woman because her grandchildren did not get to see her very often. Transportation was a problem; I was about ten before we owned a car. I can't recall a time when we rode in a buggy to visit Grandma. I enjoyed watching Grandma milk her pet goat as the goat munched on grass cuttings from a little table. If Grandma ever told me stories about her life or baked cookies for the grandchildren, I simply don't remember that.

Searching for the Truth

The Vow
"A vow does not begin a life of rigid adherence
to a set of laws;
rather a vow breaks any rigid set of laws in our life.
A vow stimulates us to risk growth
in God's spiritual way of life.
A vow binds us to a higher law—
God's law of love and truth
which demands dependence on God."
(John Dear)

My search for the truth began when I enrolled in the first grade in a two- room school called Lost Canyon, Codell. Eagerly I applied myself to the lessons in reading, unlocking words on a page. I learned to sight-read because phonics had not yet become popular. I discovered the world of numbers when I could prove with little sticks that two plus two did indeed and always would add up to four. I learned to make pencil marks on the page and, and if I arranged them correctly, I could form words that I could read.

All this and much more made my days in first grade an interesting search for the truth and the start of my great romance with books. As I moved along into the world of science, history, and geography, I dreamed of someday making a trip around God's great world in order to witness first-hand the wonders I was learning about in my little two-room schoolhouse. I graduated from that school in the spring of 1932, and entered the Dominican Sisters' postulancy the same summer. There I began and completed my high school under the direction of very capable Sister teachers, and the kind guidance of my postulant and novice director, Sister

Augustine Haefele, who initiated me into the meaning of being a Dominican.

After teaching from 1937 to 1939 in grades one and two in Holy Family School in Odin, I then began college work. I spent the school year of 1939 to 1940 in Wichita studying in Sacred Heart College (now Newman University). It was a good time to be in college and with the help of my Dominican classmates, I made successful first steps into the land of higher learning.

That year was followed by many years of teaching in elementary classrooms, but usually in most summers I was enrolled in summer school classes where I earned bachelor's and master's degrees. These are the colleges where I studied in the summers in the field of education: Alverno in Milwaukee; Marymount in Salina (BA degree); University of Notre Dame in Notre Dame (MA); University of Kansas in Lawrence; Sacred Heart in Wichita; Fort Hays State College; and Marquette University in Marquette. I took a sabbatical in Marillac in St. Louis in 1971-1972. Following my sabbatical, my summer studies (1974, 1976, 1978, and 1981) were focused on library science and literature.

It is with a deep sense of gratitude that I had all these opportunities for higher education, and I was blessed to find avenues of enrichment wherever I went. But memories of my summers at Notre Dame stand out as most special. It was there that I felt I was walking on holy ground. The environment was peaceful and beautiful, with a spacious church and many little chapels and shrines in various areas. One author called Notre Dame a benediction, a blessing of grace and community. I have to agree with the author because I found Notre Dame to be a place where God had spoken and continues to speak. I found statues, crosses, a basilica, quiet places to be solitary, murals, Stations of the Cross, a grotto dedicated to Our Lady, plus ducks and geese and green grass. Students of other faiths and those of no faith, those in various stages of belief ...all were welcomed. The sense of community which I experienced made study an avenue of contentment and peace. God could easily be welcomed in the dining room and in the classrooms, in the dorms and in the lounges. It was easy for God and for me to feel at home at Notre Dame.

My search for truth continues while I as a Dominican Sister of Peace study the best in spiritual literature and attempt to keep up with world events through television and the internet.

An Early Call and a Prompt Response

CONTEMPLATIVE
"We become contemplatives
when God discovers Himself in us."

As a small child I expressed the wish that I might become a religious Sister and dedicate my life to God. My parents were very supportive of my wish and encouraged me in every way. At family meals the topic was often discussed, but the big question was "Where shall I become a Sister?" The only Sisters I knew were the Sisters of St. Agnes who were present in Hays, Victoria, Catherine, and in several other nearby communities. But their Motherhouse was so far away in Fond du Lac, Wisconsin! The thought of leaving family and going so far away frightened me even though I did have a cousin, Sister Marcella Wasinger, in that community. On one of her home visits, she invited me to accompany her back to the Fond du Lac Motherhouse. I hesitated. I already had three cousins in the Dominican convent in Great Bend, Sisters Norberta, Henrietta, and Isabel Miller.

Great Bend won out, and I soon began making plans to enter the postulancy at age fourteen. My pastor, Father Norman, helped me complete the necessary documents and Mama worked on my wardrobe. Entrance date was set for the Feast of St. Dominic, August 4, 1932. A beautiful summer day dawned on that important day as my parents prepared me for the trip to Great Bend. Before leaving my home, Papa asked me to kneel for his blessing. How precious for me to have this last gesture of love and deep faith as I left home! After Papa blessed me, he went to the kitchen to cry aloud in grief for my departure, and in thanksgiving he and Mama had been given a daughter whom they could dedicate to God.

After we arrived at the Motherhouse in Great Bend, I was taken up as a postulant before the statue of Our Lady while the choir sang a hymn to her and the lovely song, "Oh Thou Virgin Happy Bride." I was given a short black veil, and a medal of St. Dominic which I wore over my short black cape. I was told later that Papa cried all during this ceremony.

Being introduced to life as a postulant was not easy. I found the early rising at five o'clock and long morning prayer and something that was called a thirty-minute meditation tiring. I didn't have a clue what meditation was all about. Early mornings for me meant being out in God's good fresh air, not in a stuffy non-air-conditioned chapel. Many an early morning, I felt sick but I didn't dare express this to our postulant mistress, Sister Augustine Haefele, for fear I would be sent home. Our postulant class experienced difficulties in praying in Latin. We were reciting Latin psalms several times a day, never having a clue what the words meant. (I am eternally grateful that Vatican II promoted prayer in the vernacular!)

High school classes began and I was soon in the midst of an algebra class which I found confusing and pure nonsense. Sister Thomasine Schuetz tried her best to make me understand that z's and x's do have worth and meaning, but that didn't stop the flow of my tears which appeared at times when I simply just didn't get it!!!

I waited many summers when I was in college to enroll in a required algebra class. I waited until a less exacting teacher was assigned for the course. And to my own surprise, at that time I learned the value of x and y and even z! But I often wondered just what value that knowledge would have for me when I became a teacher.

Besides the usual high school classes, there was also manual work to be done in the convent and on the grounds. Our mistress, Sister Augustine, had come from a high class family in Germany and had never done physical work. But our class had known what work meant back home and we fit in quite well for the physical work that was required. We tended gardens, gathered produce, helped in meal preparations, did laundry work, and kept all areas of the convent sparklingly clean. What a blessing to have a comedian in our class in the person of Sister Mildred Marie Eakes; she helped us in many a tight spot to see the comical in daily life and enjoy hearty laughter!

Investing day for the nine of us postulants arrived on March 27, 1933. Our class had made an eight day retreat, my first retreat. A silent retreat was the ideal although we nine didn't always measure up to that criteria. There was much excitement in the air; we just had to talk a little bit. The Dominican habit and the promise of a new name, to be called Sister, to begin a serious year called a Novitiate year in which our primary purpose was to be involved in religious training... this was in store for our group. As was the custom, each postulant had to present herself to the local bishop, Bishop August Schwertner at the time, the day before the day of investiture. As he glanced at my papers during my visit, he noted that I had not been confirmed. That had to be attended to before I could receive the habit, so on March 26, 1933, I was confirmed; my sister Amelia was my sponsor. The reason I had not been confirmed was that when the bishop came for confirmation on his last five year visit in our parish, I was too young to be confirmed. My 1933 record was to have been kept at St. Rose Parish, but as I learned a few years ago, that was neglected. However, now my confirmation record has been inserted in the community's archives in Great Bend. I was honored to have my beloved family present for my first big day in the convent.

It took me some time to get used to wearing the long white religious habit, the belt and the rosary, complete with a tight fitting cover of my head, and a white veil. Then began the year of intense training in the proper way to be a Sister. Our views as simple little novices were not considered important and hence they were never asked for by our superiors nor offered. Our class did however continue to study the regular high school subjects, plus special religious classes. We were taught about the vows which we hoped to pronounce in two years. At that time there was little written on how to be a Sister, so I couldn't just find the right book and absorb all I would need to know to be an intelligent professed religious. Sister Augustine did her best to train us, but as I look back on those days in 1933 and 1934, I wish there had been at least a few books for my enlightenment.

The next two years passed quickly as I prepared to make vows of poverty, celibacy, and obedience. At that time obedience meant to do everything I was told without questioning. The voice of the superior was considered to be the voice of God; I tried my best to take this very seriously. Poverty meant that I didn't own anything, would live with as little as possible, and would be dependent on the community for all my needs; I was not to cling to a series of wants. According to poverty and obedience, I was to learn to ask the superior's permission for many things, most of which I thought were trivial matters. Holiness meant doing the little things well, not searching for valiant deeds such as martyrdom. Celibacy meant I took Jesus for my spouse and would never marry nor be involved in intimate close relationships with any human.

On that important day, August 20, 1935, after a second eight-day retreat, I pronounced my temporary vows, making profession as a Dominican Sister. "For one year" we were told to say, but in my heart I had no hesitation and I knew this was the day I was calling on God to accept my fidelity and keep me as His own "until death."

As I remember my first year of profession, our class remained in the Novitiate under the direction of Sister Augustine. I still had some high school classes to complete before I would graduate. During that year 1935 to 1936, I completed high school and also did some daily work in the laundry. I found the laundry work especially difficult and I was often very exhausted and felt light-headed. I also had problems with my wrists which left me with little strength. I once had a fainting spell in the chapel after I had worked all morning in the laundry. Eventually a doctor discovered that I was a chronic anemic patient and I was put on an iron regime. A doctor's checkup? I never had had one but after these episodes, I had regular check-ups and received the needed iron in my blood.

Nineteen thirty-seven came at last. I was about to fulfill my second life-long dream. My first was fulfilled when I became Sister Alvina. My second dream was on the horizon...to become a teacher. With that dream came a two-day written testing time, tests that covered seventeen subjects. I shouted my Alleluia when I was told that I had passed the test and was qualified to begin teaching!

Classrooms, children, here I come!

Initiation Time: My First Teaching Assignment

You DOMINICAN women are called to contemplate
the presence of God everywhere
-in the Word of Scripture
-in the Wisdom of Creation
-in beauty, truth, and justice
-in sacramental daily living
-in our brothers and sisters
-in the eagle, the violet, the child
-in the most forgotten and neglected
-in the events of our times
-in the church
-in the communion of the faithful ones.
YOU ARE CALLED
to live and to give the fruit of this CONTEMPLATION

It was August of 1937, when I stepped into the room that was to be my classroom. I had passed the two days of intense testing and was deemed ready to teach first- and second-graders in Holy Family School in Odin, Kansas. I recall that I was entrusted with about two dozen children. In truth I really knew very little about teaching, but there were manuals to help me. I felt that the pastor, Father Nicholas Niederpreum, was leery about my abilities to teach the ordinary studies, like reading, writing, and numbers; could he expect that I would be capable of preparing second graders for first reconciliation and first Communion? I was intent on doing my best and I felt good about the results, even though teachers at that time seldom received praise or thanks for jobs well done, but were often reprimanded if we erred. From the beginning I learned that the only praise or thanks I could expect was from my God.

The two-story Holy Family School building was of native stone and contained eight classrooms; elementary classes were on first floor and the high school classrooms were on second. The elementary teachers were Sisters Alberta Neises, Raphael Husmann, Mildred Steinke, and myself. Sisters Joseph Tockert and Immaculata Penka taught in the high school. Mother Bona Silberhorn was principal for the entire school. Sisters Jordan Rziha and Raymond Brau were our faithful housekeepers.

In those days it was the common custom to have frequent Requiem Masses celebrated during the week. It was the task of Sister Alberta and me to bring the large dark candlesticks from the balcony and place them next to the catafalque. On one occasion, we didn't do this to Father's satisfaction and when he came there to bless the catafalque, he muttered, "Next time I will do it myself!" However, the records show that he never did!

There were comical incidents from my days in the Odin parish. One little acolyte dropped a flaming taper and refused to step on it to extinguish the flame. When questioned, he said, "I thought it was blessed." On one Holy Saturday morning when the pastor was blessing the vat of water, he noticed that there was something in the water. He questioned the server, "What is it?" The lad replied, "A fish." It was discovered to be a part of the decoration from the Easter candle.

For some strange reason the pastor demanded that the shades in the classrooms be drawn every evening. If anyone of us neglected to do that, we heard from him, "She can pack her trunk and go home." At times we Sisters felt like we were having a second novitiate, so strict was the pastor.

My two years in Odin was followed by a year of college work at Sacred Heart College (Newman University) in Wichita. There were five Sisters who lived in the tiny crowded house on South Millwood; Sister Benigna Albers was the superior. The students were Sisters Alfreda Thieme, William Hipp, Alexia Stremel, and I. Our little house was seldom heated or cooled to our satisfaction. We just had to learn "to offer up our discomfort for the poor souls."

I recall that we were scheduled to take a rhetoric class taught by Sister Clementine C.S.J. None of us had any idea what the word rhetoric even meant; Sister was not slow in enlightening us. She taught us how to write term papers and how to use reference books. She warned us not to take ideas out of context. For example, one might read in the Bible "Judas went out and hanged himself." She warned us not to connect that to what we found a few pages later which reads, "Go and do likewise."

My first year in college was completed, but there were many more years in colleges and in summer schools until I had the required degrees and educational abilities which were needed for my diverse ministries.

My Ministry as Classroom Teacher

DOMINICAN MOTTO
Contemplata aliis trader
To contemplate and give to others
the fruits of CONTEMPLATION

St. Leo in St. Leo, Kansas

After that eventful year in Sacred Heart College, I was assigned in 1940, to teach the first and second grades in St. Leo, a small country school in Kingman County. Sister Nicholas Tockert served as superior, principal, and teacher of grades seven and eight. Sister Caroline Oeding taught grades five and six, and Sister Evelyn Gunzelman taught third- and fourth-graders. My cousin Sister Isabel Miller was our housekeeper.

Our elderly pastor was Father Albrecht Kienhoefer, who died during my time in St. Leo. We learned some of his strange antics, such as his somewhat strange driving habits. When he would come to a stop sign, he would simply honk his horn and proceed through the intersection, as if to say, "Get out of my way; here I come." On one occasion when he had gone to Great Bend to attend an investiture ceremony at the Motherhouse, we asked him later how everything went. "Everything was mixed up. They even had ice cream on top of the pie!"

After Father's death on January 28, 1941, St. Leo had several priests from the Wichita Diocese serving the parish for various short periods of time. One priest from Holland seemed to be very strange; parents questioned his habit of frightening girls. This priest also liked to spend Saturday afternoons in our parlor listening to opera; his radio was not working well, he said. It was inconvenient to have him in our parlor all afternoon; Sister Isabel solved our problem when she figured out how to disconnect our radio so it didn't work either. After his departure from St. Leo, it became clear that he was not an ordained priest but an imposter.

Just two years after his ordination, Father Robert Herklotz replaced the foreign priest; he proved to be a breath of fresh air in the parish. He was good with the children and the parishioners were also pleased with Father Herklotz.

St. Mary School in Garden City

After being in St. Leo for one year, I was assigned to St. Mary School in Garden City from 1941 to 1946. At that time, this was a very poor parish which years before had started the construction of the parish school and then had to let the project lie idle for several years for lack of funds. When a World War II air base came to the area, many people got jobs and their income made possible the completion of the school in 1941. Our pastor, Father George Spaeth, was elated when the debt was finally paid and the school could be opened.

There was a double challenge for the Sister teachers who opened St. Mary School that fall; many of the children were Mexican and could not speak English. Besides inadequate prior educational opportunities, there was the language barrier with which we had to contend. In my classroom there were about thirty first graders who taught me a bit of Spanish; hopefully I taught them much about the English language. I held that position for three years, and then Sister Regina Leiker took over grade one, and I progressed to teaching third-graders. One of my students was

Antoinette Geier, who later became Sister Jolene in my Dominican community.

During my time in Garden City, I learned what World War II rationing meant. Sugar and flour were two food stuffs on the ration list, but also there was the rationing of rubber. What difference did it make to me if rubber was rationed? The synthetic substance that was on the bottom of the boys' shoes was often a matter of irritation to the Sisters who would spend hours on Saturdays removing the black marks on the floor of the sanctuary. It seemed to delight the servers to try to outwit each other in getting the most marks on the floor.

My assignment to Garden City made it clear that I was to be a teacher of grade one. But besides teaching there were many other duties that came my way. Another Saturday duty was the job of counting the children's Sunday collection. Pennies and pennies, hundreds of them...all had to be counted and wrapped. We Sisters were often involved on Saturdays and even Sundays in teaching religion to those children not attending St. Mary School. This included children from farming areas, from Holcomb , Syracuse, Lakin, Ingalls, and Deerfield.

Early on, I learned that teaching school also meant many other duties, all accomplished for a meager fifty dollars a month as salary. Since an average school month had twenty days, I was being paid about $2.50 a day. A school day averaged at least eight hours; that would be about $.30 an hour. If God's honor and glory was not my motive, I was indeed a foolish virgin. I never forgot that I was carved on the hand of God and that made possible my long hours and hard work above the call of duty. In those days of much labor and little pay, I was grateful that God had blessed me with a clear mind and healthy body, and an eagerness to carry the Gospel wherever I was called.

In 1951, I was again assigned to St. Mary School in Garden City where I taught first grade for one year. I do not remember any special events of that year except the surprise that came my way in the spring of 1952, when Sister Augustine, hospital administrator, had a heart attack. I was asked to take charge of St. Catherine Hospital business office. I had this position for a year.

In August of 1953, I was back at St. Mary School teaching first grade. The Sisters had moved into a new convent and the school enrollment had multiplied. The children in grades one and two had small classrooms in the basement of the convent. About thirty children were crowded into each of these rooms. That year we initiated Parent-Teacher conferences and home visits to the children's homes. Sometimes that was a problem because we had to walk to the various homes, and at times encountered dogs on the way. Frequently the parents were at work when we arrived, but some parents did come for classroom visits which was a profitable venture. I left St. Mary School in the spring of 1955.

St. Francis Xavier School, Seward

It was August of 1946, when I was sent to Seward to teach the first four grades. This was quite an uneventful year as I remember; in my books I would call it dull. Our pastor, Father Leonard Torline, suffered from sleeping sickness and was known to fall asleep in an instant. We wondered sometimes if he was listening to what we were telling him about something we needed done.

St. Rose School, Great Bend

In 1947, I was assigned to teach grade three at St. Rose School in Great Bend. There were enough children that each grade had its own classroom. During that year Father James Tainter left his Jesuit community and joined the Diocese of Wichita. When he was assigned to St. Rose, he often visited the children and shared many of his missionary adventures. From a great hurricane which he survived, he showed pictures and told of the terrible tragedy in which many were killed and much property was damaged.

During those two years that I taught in St. Rose, we teachers lived at the Motherhouse and drove daily to our school. This arrangement was inconvenient because we Sister teachers were expected to follow the daily schedule of the Motherhouse, as well as the school schedule.

From 1958 to 1960, I was again at St. Rose teaching first grade. My class was placed in an upstairs room and the little ones had to use the fire escape to enter and leave the building. I always considered this as very dangerous but because Sister Annunciata Schreiner who was advanced in years was given a room on the first floor, I was moved to second floor. A new state regulation made it necessary that after fifteen years as teacher, we were required to do three weeks of practice teaching in the presence of a supervisor. I fulfilled that requirement in the summer of 1960, and wonder even to this day why that was so necessary.

St. Peter School, Willowdale

From 1949 to 1951, I taught in a public school district in Willowdale, in which all the students were from St. Peter Parish. There I had grades three and four in a four- room school. Religion had to be taught before the regular school day began at 9:00 a.m. There I did receive a higher salary, the same salary offered to teachers in all the district's public schools.

St. Boniface School, Sharon

I had my first experience as principal from 1955 to 1958 in the three-teacher St. Boniface School in Sharon, where I served for three years as teacher of first and second grades. Our school building was a very old building which lacked indoor plumbing. The children had outdoor restrooms and we Sisters had to walk a block to our home for bathroom facilities. Sister Isabel Weber taught third and fourth grades, and Sister Edith Marie Hauser taught grades six, seven, and eight. We had to provide our own janitorial service, even scrubbing the wooden floors with water that had to be carried to the rooms.

For the most part I found our pastor, Father Wenzel Birzer, very hard to please. If something was out of order, he would reprimand publicly, whether that was in school or in church. Perhaps the children, according to him, walked too slowly or too fast, or the music was not according to his pleasure, he would make his comments a matter of open display.

The parish was in the process of building a new four-room school, and because my teaching certificate was only good for principalship for a three-room school, I had to be replaced.

After I became qualified as principal, I was called to return to Sharon from 1964 to 1966. The enlarged school now had four classrooms, and since we didn't have enough Sisters to staff the school, the parish hired a lay teacher. A new convenient convent was also built and we no longer had to go a full block to find a restroom. However, the Sisters continued to clean the school until under a government plan, we were able to hire young people who were considered to be poor. Monsignor Joseph Stremel was thanked for securing this important assistance to teachers. The Sisters did not have a car and when they needed to go some place, they had to ask some generous parishioner for the use of a car.

Our Lady of the Assumption School, Pueblo, Colorado

For the first time in my teaching career, I was assigned out of Kansas, namely to Pueblo, Colorado, from 1960 to 1961. I had forty students in my classroom, and had no access to aides. Many students were of Italian or Mexican descent, and in the parish this ethnicity was very evident. The Italians had their special dinners, the Mexicans had theirs, and the Americans had theirs. I found the parishioners very generous and supportive of the school. The Sisters often enjoyed meals of fresh trout given by the folks. Churches were never crowded except on Easter when Mass had to be celebrated in the courtyard.

The people in the city of Pueblo suffered from the smog given off by the many factories which produced carbon. Our white habits were difficult to keep clean because the dust clung to the mohair material.

On one weekend we Sisters decided to go for a little vacation to a cabin owned by the diocese. Sister Diane Traffas directed the driver and we found the cabin without any problems. We unpacked the car, put everything into the cabin, even the car keys. The cabin door shut when we left and lo and behold, we found we were locked out!!! We couldn't drive any place to get help for the car keys were locked safely inside the cabin. We examined the windows and found one slightly ajar. Praise God! Since Sister Catherine was the smallest Sister among us, she was chosen to climb through the window. She got halfway in and then we all burst into giggles. There she was hanging half in and half out. Eventually we pushed her the rest of the way in; she retrieved the cabin keys, and we were SAFE!!!

During my year in Pueblo, my brother Arthur and his German wife Maria came to visit me from their home in El Paso, Texas. My brother was in the army and was stationed in Fort Bliss, Texas. That also was the year in which my cousin Leota's little five year old, Beverly, died of acute leukemia. I was not able to attend the funeral, but I wrote her a letter which she kept for many years because it had brought her so much comfort. "Sister, you were the one who helped me in this time of grief," Leota told me.

Here is the message that I sent to Leota, Bob, and family on November 13th, 1960:

> It grieves me greatly to have heard about the loss of your little one. For reasons known only to God have you tended the garden of your family. I know you have done and tried to do what is right. Crosses and trials come in any state of life but we must trust in God when all seems in vain. Like any gardener you have planted the seed, you have waited for its growth, you have tended it with care, and have watched and delighted in its beauty. The soul of little Beverly was the most beautiful in your family garden. Again like the earthly gardener gathers the

most beautiful flowers so the Divine Gardener has looked upon your garden and has seen the soul of Beverly to be the most beautiful, so in His delight He has gathered her home to adorn His home with another of His innocent souls. Yes, it grieves me to see one taken from the family but "God has given and God has taken; blessed be the name of the Lord." Only in eternity will we know the reasons. But while we live here in this land of exile we must pray daily for a deep faith in the loving Providence of God. I have been praying for you since I heard last Monday evening....I will continue to pray for you that this cross that God has seen to give you will make you stronger in clinging to His holy will.

St. Peter School, Schulte

My assignment in 1961-1962, was to St. Peter School in Schulte, near Wichita. The school building was very old and too small. There were four classrooms and a library; I taught grades three and four. One of my students was a second cousin, Michelle Seachris. The church also was very small and the pastor was in the process of planning a larger church; it seems he had it placed in an unfavorable location and it was not made large enough for the rush of Wichita people moving westward. As Wichita expanded to the west, Schulte received many of the folks from west Wichita. A new larger school building was soon built after I left, and also a larger church. At the end of that school year, the pastor was changed and also the Sisters.

School of the Magdalen, Wichita

From 1962 to 1964, I was assigned to teach the sixth grade in the School of the Magdalen, my first adventure with sixth graders. My forty students had travelled over many parts of the world and this presented a challenge for me. They never knew how terrified I was in this environment. Nearly every day there was a High Mass in the old church, which was really the school auditorium. At Christmas the pastor, Monsignor George Schmidt, gave the Sunday choir members tickets to see the ice capades. The Sisters protested; the children had sung nearly every morning and we thought we Sisters were entitled to tickets also. Our protests bore fruit and the Sisters received tickets.

After I left the School of the Magdalen, the parish built a circular church which later had to be demolished in order to widen Kellogg Street. The parish plant is now located in the northeastern part of Wichita.

St. Michael School, LaCrosse

Father Jacob Dreher was pastor when I went to LaCrosse in 1966 to be principal and to teach third and fourth graders. I found that he was very talented with wood and other materials. He had made all the Christmas decorations, and he was very cooperative in school matters. I recall he brought a black widow spider to show the children and to warn them of the danger of being bitten by such a spider. Father George McLaughlin replaced Father Dreher after a year and a half. Sister Rosemary Mauler taught the first and second graders, Benny Viegra taught fifth and sixth, and Sister Roseanne Penka taught seventh and eighth grades.

Because of financial difficulties, St. Michael School was in danger of being closed. At the end of my third (or was it second?) year in LaCrosse, the final decision was eventually made. The public school district rented the building the following year; Benny Viegra and Sister Rosemary continued to teach in the public school for the following year.

Sacred Heart School, Sapulpa, Oklahoma

From 1968 to 1971, I was teaching outside of Kansas; I was assigned to Sacred Heart School in Sapulpa, Oklahoma. There I was principal and teacher of the fifth and sixth grades. The school had grades one through six, plus kindergarten. Two lay teachers were hired, one to teach kindergarten and the other third and fourth graders. It took me some time to get used to the southern accent. A lady was hired to keep the school clean.

The church was three blocks from the school, so Father Murthau celebrated daily Mass in the extra classroom. From this school we were able to take the fifth and sixth graders for a number of field trips.

We toured the Oklahoma City zoo, the National Cowboy Hall of Fame, the Cosmosphere, some museums, the Harry Truman library, a museum in Missouri, the Will Rogers museum, and a Cherokee Indian village in Tahlequah. At this village, a guide shared some interesting facts about how Indians live. This village is staffed with Cherokees living and performing much like their ancestors did some three hundred years ago. During the months of June and July, there is an outdoor performance of "The Trail of Tears." Since our visit there was not in the summer months, we missed this spectacular performance.

It was a sad day when I heard that the Dominican Sisters could no longer staff Sacred Heart School. If the parish wanted to keep the school open, they would have to hire a lay staff. I had come to dearly love the children and the families, and it was with deep sadness that I said goodbye. I felt like I was between two forces, community saying I had to leave, and the parishioners being resentful that we were leaving. The School Board gave us the car we had been using, and Sister Amata Pantel and I drove it home. The other two Sisters had already gone to Great Bend.

A lady who often cleaned the school left this message on the board on our last day:

> Silent tears filled my eyes
> I could but barely realize
> The words that had been spoken:
> This school is soon to close.
> One man's dream of a place for
> his flock to learn
> Has become another heartache and pain
> For reality today---Follow the trend
> Another "Era" has come to an end!

With the closing of the school in Sapulpa came the end of my teaching career, as I began to look into the possibility of becoming a librarian in parochial schools. I would still be ministering to children but in a different capacity.

Dear God, I know You have my name carved in the palm of Your hand. Now I ask You to heal my hurting heart as I leave a school and ministry that I love so much.

Opportunities for Enriching Body, Soul, and Spirit

CELIBACY
"Celibacy- a vacancy for God
To be empty for God
To be free and open for His presence
To be available for His service."
(St. Thomas Aquinas)

Sabbatical at Marillac

After many years as classroom teacher, the closing of Sacred Heart School in Sapulpa, and the death of my beloved Papa, my spirits were beginning to sag in 1971, and I felt the need of some enrichment. I requested a sabbatical and was given a year of study at Marillac College in St. Louis, Missouri. Marillac was a Catholic inter-community liberal arts college conducted by the Sisters of Charity of St. Vincent. I found that the purpose of the college was to provide educational and professional preparation for religious women.

The Sisters initiated a one year Theology Renewal Program which contemporizes Sisters in professional and religious orientation, especially those who had known only pre-Vatican theology. The faculty, both religious and lay, taught theology which could be used for both elementary and secondary levels. The college drew professors from St. Louis University, Kenrick Seminary, and Cardinal Glennon College, which added to the enriched environment in which I saturated myself for about nine months.

I was in admiration of the spirit among the Sisters at Marillac. I found them to be interested in each other, kind to each other, and living their unspoken motto of LIVE AND LET LIVE. There were many opportunities for spiritual renewal. The daily liturgies were meaningful; there were many weekend workshops like one called "TheThree C's (Care, Concern, Compassion)". There were ways to confront contemporary moral problems, sessions on how to prepare for retirement, and sessions on pastoral ministry. I recall one special liturgy which included a communal penance service, times for reflection, a special Thanksgiving Vespers, all culminating in the liturgy of the Eucharist. This eventful liturgy was followed by a wonderful banquet and a talent show.

Physical enrichment came from: my frequent walks on the lovely campus; playing tennis, volley ball, basketball, and ping pong; and taking bicycle rides. Culturally there were many varied and wonderful activities in St. Louis; I had to make my choices for there were more than one person could attend.

I describe my sabbatical year as a time when I experienced meaningful human contacts with many wonderful Sisters. In the Theology Renewal Program Sisters' ages ranged from twenty-four to sixty. They came from various states and various professions. I was among nurses, dietitians, teachers, formation directresses, and contemplative perpetual adoration Sisters.

As my spiritually motivated year was drawing to a close, I was musing over where my ministry might lead me. I thought of working in a media-center library, or do individualized teaching, or teach religion to those who are nine years or older. I had the happy surprise of an invitation from Sister Diane Traffas, asking me to consider being librarian at the School of the Magdalen in Wichita.

A Summer in a House of Prayer

With the enthusiasm and encouragement which was so typical of Father Bernard Haring C.Ss.R., many religious communities turned their attention to establishing houses of prayer in the sixties and seventies. Sister Malachy Stockemer and I from the Great Bend community volunteered to attend a six weeks house of prayer experience in Kentucky. I learned some important information about prayer, even though I never became a part of a House of Prayer group.

We flew to Louisville. There we were separated into groups of four, five, or six persons, depending on the size of the house to which we were assigned. I lived with four Sisters in a small convent of the parish called Hope. This was four miles from the Gethsemini Monastery of the Trappist monks. We attended daily Mass in their chapel; however, we had to remain in the choir and were not allowed in the monastery. Our eighty member group of Sisters was invited on the feast of the Visitation to enter the monastery for the Mass and to enjoy a picnic with the monks.

On weekends we went to Louisville where we participated in theology sessions given by very famous theologians in that area. I remember two speakers in particular, Brother David Rast, and a Father Hennessey. These six weeks were a profitable time for me, plus I had the privilege of being with Trappists.

The Two Hundred Dollar Trip with Memories to Last a Lifetime

In July of 1981, it was my great joy to join a group of thirteen sixty-year- old Sisters for a vacation to Nebraska, South Dakota, and Wyoming. We had the good fortune to participate in this great adventure because of the generosity and foresight of Sister Eloise Hertel and Mickey Wasinger. The group consisted of Sisters Baptista Luebbers, Monica Staudinger, Bernice Wenke, Josephine and Stanislaus Blazek, Damian Schreiner, Michael Schwarzenberger, Catherine Miller, Leocadia Rachbauer, Amata Pantel, Seraphine Grabbe, and me. Our navigator was Sister Malachy Stockemer.

Fortified by the prayer and good wishes of the Sisters at the Motherhouse, we boarded the comfortable fifteen passenger van, named Voyager with its BT 1425 tag at 8:00 a.m. on July 21. All our luggage plus a birthday cake rested under the seats. We moved through Hays and headed for Plainville as we prayed the Rosary. There was a brief restroom stop in Stockton, and soon we were noticing the sign that read Nebraska. At noon we stopped at Holdrege for lunch at the Hotel Dale. Beginning at that stop and at most of the stops thereafter, folks took notice of the large group of traveling Sisters. One lady said, "The church is here, come in."

Our first overnight stop along Highway 80 was at a Motel 6 in North Platte, Nebraska, where we caught our breath, found our rooms (four to a room), sang some songs, rested a bit, watched TV for a while, prayed Evening Praise, and enjoyed supper at Howard Johnson's. There was also a birthday to celebrate, Sister Michael's. We shared the cake which Sister Alvarita Brungardt had graciously baked for the occasion.

After a restful night, we were up by 6:00 a.m. in order to attend the 7:00 o'clock Mass at St. Patrick's twelve blocks away. After the Mass, the pastor came to greet us and find out what these Dominican Sisters were up to. We ate breakfast at McDonald's and then settled into the van for our trip to Rapid City in South Dakota, some three hundred miles away. Our Morning Praise was accompanied by thunder and lightning even as we watched the beauties of God's handiwork in nature. We had a mid-morning break at Thedford where we exchanged seats. Along the way, we enjoyed snacks of peanuts, sunflower seeds, wheat thins, and gum drops. We changed our clocks to mountain time before coming to Rapid City.

Soon we began marveling at the beauties of the Badlands in the Badland Memorial National Park. To me it looked like God had dug a deep hole, pulled up large pieces of the earth, only to turn it upside down for a mountain, all done with a gorgeous array of colors. It was a good opportunity to take pictures of this beautiful splash of colors. We drove on to Rapid City where we again stayed at a Motel 6. We ate supper at the Big Chief, and later in the evening were refreshed with soft drinks, Coors, and pretzels.

On July 23, we were warned that the travel would cover many miles. After breakfast at the Big Chief, we headed for Mount Rushmore. At Keystone we stopped and bought cards and some bought ice cream. We were thrilled by the beauty in that area, and we recognized the skill of the artists who had brought four national heroes to life. After taking pictures, we moved on to Crazy Horse Mountain. We were served lunch in cowboy style at Dakota Cowboy Café.

Eagerly we were looking forward to the great treat of the trip, namely the opportunity to be present at the famous Passion Play near Spearfish, Wyoming. We drove through red hills like those in Sharon, Kansas, and we arrived at Devil's Tower. This tower is said to be the tallest rock formation in the States. The tip of the mountain is flat; the base is about one thousand feet in diameter. The pasture ground sloping up toward the mountain is a town of prairie dogs.

 After our meal and a stop at the motel, we drove to the area of the Passion Play. Happily we had front row seats to watch this marvelous display of talent honoring the last days of Jesus. Prancing white horses, flocks of sheep, and three camels made the performance seem so real. At the crucifixion scene, God provided a display of lightning and thunder, but the rain held off until we were safely inside. To say that the play was a marvel is putting it mildly; words cannot describe the emotions I experienced while I watched the enactment of the passion.

On July 24th, we were ready to begin the long trip home. We stopped at Spearfish, North Platte, Kodoka, Gothenberg, Norton, WaKeeney, and Ness City before being welcomed at Great Bend at about 5:00 p.m. It was a nice surprise when Mickey handed each of us a fifty dollar bill; the cost of the trip had been estimated as costing each of us $200, but our cost was only $150 apiece.

Tired and worn, each of us gave praise to God for this splendid experience, which will not soon be forgotten.

God's Graciousness in 1985

There were two extraordinary blessings from God that came my way in 1985, namely the celebration of my fifty years of religious profession and the opportunity to make a thirty-day Ignatian retreat in Sedalia, Colorado. A Dominican making an Ignatian retreat? Yes, as I immersed myself in the daily prayer and reflection times, I came to see that this type of retreat matched my temperament. I am an SJ on the Myers-Briggs scale, which means that I have a deep sense of obligation and always want to feel useful. SJ's are givers rather than receivers, caring for those in need, and wanting to contribute to the good of society. According to the focus of this retreat, one is encouraged to ponder Scripture as if it were happening today, and then to reflect on how it fits into my life presently.

I was led through this experience by my director, Sister Eleanor Sheehan CSJ, with whom I met on a daily basis. Sister led me through an adventure of addressing each family member and eliciting the feelings I had toward them and they might have toward me. I was still feeling an aloneness because only one family member had come to Great Bend for the recent celebration of my golden jubilee of profession. Sharing this hurt with Sister was helpful in healing that hurt. I felt that in a way I was washing feet like Jesus did. There were tears at times, but the tears were tears of healing when I learned that I cannot compare my gifts with that of others nor deem myself as inadequate. Long walks were part of the schedule and sometimes these were for four miles, providing leisure for reflection on some things in my life which I needed to relinquish.

During those thirty days, I became aware of a feeling of intimate closeness with Jesus after I received Eucharist. This precious feeling sometimes lasted for hours, or even for days. Silence was kept at all times, except for two days a month when retreatants had a chance to go away for a day, and even receive mail. On one of those days, I was blessed with a thoughtful letter from my spiritual director, Father Heim.

Sister Adeline Wedeking provided me a ride to Great Bend at the end of the retreat. What met me at the Motherhouse was a large crowd of former members who had come for a gathering we called "Remembering." It was a real shock for me to be thrust into so much chattering, after spending a month in total silence. I have the same feeling when many Sisters gather for Community Days; I enjoy greeting everyone, but there comes a time in the afternoon when I have to move into the silence of my room.

I continue to experience a deep sense of gratitude for the wonderful grace-filled thirty days of retreat in 1985, where I learned to see myself through new eyes and recognize again God's unconditional love for me.

Land of Books...Here I Come

"A balanced life of prayer, reading, Divine Office,
study, and work are important.
This embraces Lectio Divina,
the doctrinal study and meditative reading of Scripture
which will pass quickly to prayer and meditation."

My interest in library science dates back to 1952-1953 when I worked in the business office at St. Catherine Hospital in Garden City. Sister Alfonsa Schreiner was eager to learn about library work and since Fort Hays College was offering a course in library science in Garden City, the two of us enrolled and attended the Saturday morning classes. My thoughts were directed to the idea that some day I would like to work in the libraries of elementary schools. As my sabbatical came to a close, I sent a letter out to my community offering my services as librarian. Sister Diane Traffas responded and invited me to serve as librarian in the School of the Magdalen in Wichita. I accepted her invitation.

I felt a sense of fulfillment as I began teaching library science to the children in September of 1972. The children were eager to learn and were appreciative of the many stories I read to the various classes. A wide variety of children's books were on the market; this was a far cry from the scarcity of books available when I was a child. I learned about new books and new authors even as I was teaching this on a daily basis. It was an exciting time for me and I count those two years at the Magdalen as great.

In the fall of 1974, I chose to serve in St. Dominic School in Garden City. I was school secretary in the mornings and librarian in the afternoons. I had extra time during that year, and I offered Father

Ronald Renner to assist in taking Eucharist to shut-ins and to those in nursing homes. After a year as secretary and librarian, I discovered that secretarial work was not to my liking, and I began in 1975 to split my time in the libraries of the two parochial schools, St. Dominic and St. Mary. I enjoyed my work more and more each day; the faces of the little ones would beam as I read stories and shared my teaching of library science with the help of charts which I made. I kept to this schedule for two years; then in 1977 and continuing through 1980, I served only in the library in St. Mary School. I had had surgery the previous summer and needed to curtail my activities.

When I resigned as librarian in St. Dominic's school Father Renner would not accept my resignation. He told me to think it over and then decide. He did not want me to leave but that was not to be. I had to resign anyway.

During my time at St. Mary School, the building underwent a big renovation project which greatly improved the building. Electrical work, new plumbing, new carpeting, lowering of ceilings...all these improvements added to the beauty and accessibility of the school. The children were pleased with the new look and uttered many an Oh and Ah! I received special compliments from the principal for what I had done in the library:

> Sister took a Book Room and turned it into a library.
> Her planning both short- and long-range is out-
> standing. The appearance of the library is outstand-
> ing. Students are motivated to the "love of books."
> Sister takes a special pride in her work which is well
> beyond what would normally be expected...St.
> Mary's School is indebted for all she has done. She

is totally dedicated to her work. The only word I can come up with to describe the work Sister is doing is outstanding.

Through all the years I was engaged in library work, I had opportunities for study in library science, library management, and literature workshops. I became personally acquainted with authors of children's books, and found library-related workshops times of special interest and excitement. Although I never wrote a book for children, I read hundreds of them to children and watched their eyes brighten with the thrill of getting to know new peoples and areas of the world. There were library association meetings to attend, conventions which offered valuable information, computer skills to learn, and real live authors to meet. I had opportunity to meet Beverly Cleary, author of forty books for children, along with Maurice Sendak, and Dr. Seuss, plus Shel Silverstein with the lessons of *The Giving Tree*. One special three-day library meeting which I enjoyed very much was one in a hotel in Seattle, Washington. There were opportunities for a boat ride, watch salmon grilled before our eyes, enjoy delicious clam soup, and a chance to watch fishermen actually employed at their fishing occupation. On this trip I was able to make an April visit to a cousin in Marysville, Washington, forty-five minutes from our hotel. Being so far north, warm clothing felt good, but on the way home, I shed layers of clothing before arriving back in Kansas.

While in Garden City, I helped sell the World Book Encyclopedia to many families in the area. With my commission I was able to assist the African missions, and provide three sets of World Book for each of the two schools. I received the gift of a special bicentennial edition with a red, white, and blue cover; this set I used for many years before giving it to my brother's children.

In September of 1976, I was commissioned as a Communion Minister. This ministry was somewhat new and when word got around, there were many persons who wanted to assist also in this capacity. In a short time, there were as many as sixty persons who were commissioned and helped with shut-ins, patients in nursing homes, as well as distributing Eucharist at the weekend Masses in church. The sacrament was administered under both species at the Masses.

Extension of Library Science

It was in 1979 that I received an invitation from Sister Anita Schugart, administrator at St. Catherine Hospital, to develop a medical library. This was a project for which the doctors had clamored for a long time, and money had been allocated in the yearly budget. A medical library was new territory for me and I had not the slightest idea where to begin. I struggled with a type of classification suited for medical books and materials, but I was willing to give this project my very best. My work was done in a room which contained a number of medical journals which had been donated, and I soon learned the medical library classification system. By 1982, the library was scarce on space to store all the hospital records. The solution was to microfilm the records; this would save much space. Microfilm? That was a new term and experience, but I learned and with the help of a microfilming company, the monotonous work was attempted for a year.

In February of 1983, I was ready for a change of pace, and I applied as librarian to serve in the Central Kansas Medical Center in Great Bend. I started at once to clear out all outdated materials, journals, and books, and to establish order "out of chaos." Again there was a scarcity of space. I continued in that library environment until

1991, when I heard rumors of an opening in pastoral ministry in the Hoisington parish. This might be a break I needed after working in libraries since 1972.

While I was working as medical librarian at Central Kansas Medical Center, I was placed also in charge of the Motherhouse library. It was at the beginning of my time there that all the spiritual books had to be moved to a special area on second floor; the library was running out of space. In July of 1995, Heartland Center wanted their clients to have easy access to all the convent's books, so there was another move of the spiritual books from second floor back to the library. This caused much confusion for all the library cards which had already been separated into two areas had to become one set again.

Library work has its ups and downs; especially is this evident in the convent library where the top shelves are ceiling high. The library is often used for meetings and that hinders my work there; I have to work around the scheduled meetings. The library office was located in an enclosed room that had no windows and sometimes I felt like I was in a dungeon. At this writing, my office, with window access to the great outdoors, is located next to the library. This is a much appreciated space.

One of the special tasks that I especially relish is the chance to select all the new books to be ordered. Sometimes Sisters suggest titles, or I find reviews that look good, and I am free to order books within a set budget. When the books arrive, I am the first to browse or read them. Thus I become acquainted with new authors who become like new friends, and I am introduced to great sources of information. While I was ministering in Hoisington, I was also working on library cards for the Motherhouse library with a "Brother" processor. I did not have to type the new cards four or five times; the processor made the additional cards from the first card I typed. With the use of the computer, I find that the sky is the limit in getting information and new sources of knowledge, and I am pleased that library work is now computerized.

I close this section on library ministry with this quote from Father Paul Murray, O.P.:

> Let our lives be open books for all to study, a Domin-ican of the 12th century, an Englishman, had boldly suggested that the preacher's life should itself be a "book" and in that book all those who see the preacher should be able to read and study the things of God.

O God, how great Thou art in this technological age!

In the Family Circus I read the following...
"When I finish a good book, it's like a close friend just moved away."

Bil Keane

"Let our lives be open books for all to study."

Mahatma Ghandi

My Dominican Family

"The Dominican Sister is called to be a woman of vision.
She is invited to a maturity
which takes all the riches her way of life provides
and harmonizes them within the wholeness of one
who has become 'total gift' to God
and to her sisters and brothers."

The Communion of Saints... Faithful Dominicans on Earth

When I entered the postulancy on August 4th, 1932, there were few Dominican Sisters that I knew besides my three first cousins, namely Sisters Norberta, Sebastian (Henrietta), and Fridoline (Isabel). My class consisted of twelve members, ten of whom received the religious habit with me in 1933. When I celebrated my seventieth jubilee in 2005, I was the only surviving member of my class. Some had left the Dominicans; others were deceased. Again when I celebrated my 75th anniversary in 2010, I was a loner from the profession class of 1935.

I was closely associated with the eleven postulants for the next several years. We prayed and played together; we worked side by side; we made the same common mistakes as we each tried to reach for the goal of perfection set before us by our mistress, Sister Augustine Haefele. We shared times of grief and times of laughter. It was then that I began to hear Isaiah telling me that God had me in the palm of God's hand, a theme that has continued to grace me today, and given me courage in the best and worst of times. We shared the joys of investing and profession days. After first profession, our class began to scatter to various towns and cities to be ministers of the faith we loved. There were festive days of jubilee to regather when we celebrated with the entire community; there were funerals of classmates to mark end times. My community honored me especially on the days of my seventieth and seventy- fifth jubilees for I was the only member left in my class of twelve.

During Easter week of 2009, our Great Bend community was officially joined with six other groups of Dominicans to form a new congregation called Dominican Sisters of Peace. Before that date, my Great Bend community numbered about one hundred members. After the new community became official, I had about five hundred new family members, ministering in many states and in several foreign countries. With the good physical and mental health with which I am blessed, I strive to keep these Chapter commitments to the best of my ability:

1. To study, contemplate, and preach God's revelation
2. To create environments of peace by promoting nonviolence
3. To promote justice through solidarity with the marginalized
4. To create welcoming communities for new members.

The Communion of Saints... Saintly Dominicans in Heaven

St. Dominic, founder of the Order, ranks highest among my favorite Dominican Saints. I have always been inspired by his courage in establishing an Order to combat a heresy that had been the scourge of his day. He didn't hesitate to call women converts from that heresy and join them into a cloistered community whose mission was to prayerfully support the men's group that he had in mind. He sent the men to important universities that they might become versed in the best of theology and be preachers of the truth. Veritas became the motto of the Order. Dominic lived a simple life, often depriving himself of food which he gave to the poor. His books, so precious at the time, were sold for the benefit of the needy around him. The Gospel according to St. Matthew was his constant companion on the long journeys he would make in bare feet; it was said that he would put on his shoes only when going through a town.

Dominic was called a man of the Gospel. I claim him as a special friend because I too try to be a person of the Gospel. Blessed Jordan of Saxony said of Dominic: "Your strong love burned with heavenly fire and God-like zeal. With all the fervor of an impetuous heart and with an avowal of perfect poverty, you spent your whole self in the cause of the apostolic life."

I found this section from *Search for Living Waters* by Sister Miriam Scheel, OP very meaningful for me as a member of St. Dominic's family:

> From what we know of Dominic's own life and prayer the instruction of these conferences which he studied with "all the power of his mind," indeed bore fruit. Here we find a man, as witnesses tell us, who striped himself of self in a rule of poverty both regarding possessions and inner ambitions, who avoided all useless conversations in favor of speaking only about God or to God, who mourned and wept for sinners throughout the night, and preached the truth to them by day, who dialogued with God over passages of Scripture, who on his journeys sang hymns of praise for his gratuitous goodness, who pointing like an arrow set straight on

its course, allowed his spirit to ascend and contemplate mysteries reserved only for the pure of heart. Then flowing from this intense study and application he burned with extraordinary zeal; he was sturdy of mind, compassionate of heart, and everywhere he showed himself to be a man of the Gospel. Preoccupied with the necessities of administering his Order, traveling and preaching, he nevertheless carried within him the "inner mountain' of God; and like Anthony, he too became a mountain radiating the way to God exemplified in this tradition. Two followers of Dominic who saw the wisdom of this way and the wealth of the treasures hidden within were St.Thomas Aquinas (c.1225-1274) and St. Catherine of Siena (c.1347-1380).

Who would not want to admire Dominic and enter his Order?

St. Catherine was a woman of principle and for this I admire her. Catherine did what she thought was right regardless of public opinion to the contrary. She lived in an age when most women were shuttered in kitchens and convents. The unschooled Catherine, daughter of a Sienese dyer, engaged in political, social, and spiritual activism. Enflamed by her convictions and mystical devotion, she strove to restore harmony to the world. She contended with popes, monarchs, and ordinary citizens, pleading for needed reforms. She campaigned for peace among warring factions, struggled to restore unity in the church, and helped persuade Pope Gregory XI to leave Avignon and return to Rome. For all her activism, Catherine was praised and reviled, revered as a holy woman, and nearly assassinated by some of her enemies. She took a special interest in prisoners and in the sick; both groups she tended graciously, tending to their wounded hearts and bodies. Catherine died at the age of thirty-three.

St. Albert the Great is another one of my favorites, especially because he was a model teacher. In the early days of his formation, he struggled with studies of the sciences, and at one time made efforts to leave the monastery. Our Lady stopped him and reminded the lad that he had not asked her for her help. Albert returned to his cell and with Mary's help, he became one of the greatest scientists the world has ever known. I often prayed to St. Albert when I experienced difficulties in my studies.

Blessed Jane of Aza, mother of St. Dominic, had a vision before his birth. She believed she saw the son she was bearing, running as a swift hound throughout the world, carrying in his mouth a torch with which he illumined the world. My Mama had a similar experience before I was born; she told me that she felt she was bearing a child who would be very special. Was this perhaps a portent of my future call to be a religious? I like to think it was.

The Communion of Saints...the Souls in Purgatory

In my upbringing, my parents often prayed for the poor souls in purgatory. As a family we prayed for our deceased grandparents, our great and great great grandparents, plus uncles and aunts, cousins, and friends. Their names often came up in our family prayer, and Mama and Papa encouraged us to pray for the dead. It is a practice I find meaningful today, and I often pray for my former classmates in religion, as well as for the deceased members of my religious community, former students, and those to whom I have been privileged to minister. "It is a holy and wholesome thought to pray for the dead." My parents knew this and instilled this in my young mind.

Amelia and
Edmund Meis

Gloria and Cecil
Miller
(Golden Jubilee)
Mary, Arthur and
Sister Alvina

Arthur and Maria Miller

Cecil & Gloria Luea Miller

Sister Ronald Meis

With my three cousins, Sisters Isabel, Henrietta, Norberta—1932

My classmates in 1955

Sister Alvina's postulants class with Sister Augustine, 1932

Sister Alvina's first, First Communion class in Odin, KS, 1937

Sister Alvina at the grave of great-grandparents (Miller)

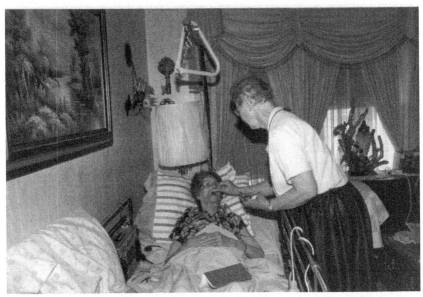

Sister Alvina bringing holy communion to patient in the hospital

Sister Alvina in the Library Office in the convent

Sister Alvina
exercising at Curves

Sisters vacationing
near Devil's Tower
in WY

My Soul Mate, a Gift from a Loving God

MENTORS
"Mentors are so important
because they have gone where we have not yet been.
They can look at us with love,
born of wisdom, grace, mercy, and compassion
and give us hints born of wisdom,
grace and mercy and compassion."

My baptismal record shows that a Capuchin priest named Father Basil Heim poured water on my head in February of 1918, and pronounced me a member of the Catholic Church. Father Heim set my feet on the path to an exciting and spirit-filled life. I believe God has a sense of humor and extremely good judgment for on December 24th, 1973, another Father Heim came into my life to offer me guidance on my journey. He was called Father Donald Heim and he came from far away Philadelphia to be chaplain at St. Catherine Hospital in Garden City. Some folks say his coming was the best thing that had happened at St. Catherine's in a long time, and Father Heim remained with us for five wonderful years.

At that time I was ministering as librarian in the two parochial schools in the city. What a blessing to assist at his noonday Mass at the hospital! Father became my confessor and spiritual director. I was especially pleased with his friendliness to everyone he met, and his way of sharing with me his own struggles as well as his successes in life. There was thus a mutual communication between us, and I came to know that I was not the only one who had difficulties in life. God had blessed me with a soul mate who remained a close friend even after he left the Dodge City diocese.

When Father Heim was given a new assignment, I missed him at the hospital but we stayed in touch through letters. He moved to Our Lady of Guadalupe in Dodge City, then to St. John in Meade and St. Patrick in Plains, then to St. Michael in LaCrosse and St. Joseph in Liebenthal. Father returned to Philadelphia in 1989, where he stayed at St. Veronica Rectory in that city and ministered on a part time basis as he was needed.

I was pleased in 1992 to receive a special invitation from Father Heim to make a visit to Philadelphia. I accepted his invitation and flew to Philadelphia for a wondrous vacation which Father had carefully planned. He met me at the airport and took me to see his home in the parish rectory. Then we went on to the Dominican Sisters Retreat Center and retirement home for the Sisters. He even took me to do a little gambling on the Showboat Casino. The trip to the Atlantic Ocean was thrilling even though it was a cloudy day. Because of Father's breathing problems, we rode in a little cart. I was honored to meet Father Joe Heim, Father Donald's brother, a missionary from Venzuela. I also met his sister who prepared a wonderful meal for us.

On Sunday, it was a joy to assist at a Mass in a German parish. Liberty Bell and a spaghetti lunch were next in line, plus a visit to Independence Hall. We visited the cathedral in which Father had been ordained in 1964. I was shown the convent of the Pink Sisters who have perpetual adoration. We rode a ferry across the Hudson River and visited a new aquarium. It was a special honor to attend Mass in the National Shrine of the Immaculate Conception and to have lunch in the basement cafeteria. We went to see the Capitol, the Vietnam Memorial, Arlington Cemetery, and Valley Forge.

On the last day of my visit east, we went to Delaware and took a ride on a barge drawn by two mules. It was threatening to rain but the buckets of rain didn't come until we were back in the car. I would liked to have stopped at a gigantic grocery store, a store so large that the employees use skates to get around, but because of the intense rain storm we didn't stop.

The whole four- day experience was pure delight, not only for the sights and sounds, but especially because I was in the presence of a holy priest, my wonderful friend, Father Donald Heim. Little did either of us realize that that would be our last time together. Father took me to the airport and I left for Kansas. We both promised to keep each other in daily prayer.
Father's health was not good for he suffered from emphysema; his smoking habits caught up with him and he died July 5th, 1994. He was buried from the church of St. Katherine of Siena in Wayne, Pennsylvania. May my dear friend, Father Donald Heim, rest in God's peace. He was the friend who helped me in many ways to attain peace.

One bit of advice I still cherish from Father Heim is: "We often long for a closeness to the Lord—but we must also yearn for the difficulties that bring us closer." His last exhortation to me on my visit in Philadelphia was: "One of Satan's angels was sent to make me suffer terribly, so that I would not feel too proud." (Cor. 12:1-10) "There is our thorn in the flesh, the thing that keeps us from developing spiritual pride. What is there that keeps us or causes us particular problems?"

Peace and deep gratitude, my dear friend, Father Heim!

Vacationing with Father Donald Heim in Philadelphia, 1993

Across the Wide Blue Atlantic

"Never domesticate the Holy"
(Bishop Ronald Gilmore)

My heart beats a little faster and some tears may fall as I remember the gifts my precious Mama gave me, especially the gift of life and a good Christian upbringing. Later in life she gave me the tremendous gift of a trip abroad. Papa and Mama had lived a frugal life and after Papa's death, Mama offered to gift me with something special because I had assisted her in many ways, especially with her finances. She made funds possible that I might travel to three continents and visit in five countries! Plans began to emerge in October of 1982, when I made a retreat with Father Jim Sheehan. I had to get a passport and that required two black and white photos which I had made in Garden City. Because my baptismal certificate had my baptismal name, I had to use Emertina on my passport.

My first step on this stupendous journey was my flight to Kennedy International Airport via St. Louis. I took a bus to KLM Terminal where I met up with the group of seventeen which formed our tour group. We boarded the Royal Jordanian for the eleven-hour trip across the Atlantic, and we landed in Amsterdam. Enroute we had been served a large midnight snack plus breakfast. We took a bus to the Schelerozad Hotel and had a short night for it was already 2:00 a.m. on August 2.

This was the day to fly to Egypt and to visit the Egyptian museum. I was amazed by the excavations and the visits in a Coptic church, a synagogue of Ben Ezra, and Sultan Hassan mosque. I expected that we would have to remove our shoes at the mosque; we didn't, but an Arab man tied canvas shoes over our shoes. I noted that the mosque had Persian rugs and crystal lights which were imported from France.

It saddened me to see the extreme poverty evident in Cairo. With a population of over eleven million people, the city has no room for appropriate housing. Many poor people sleep in parks or on roadsides. Women still wash their clothes in the river and hang them to dry at various places. The tops of many buildings were covered with junk. Along the roads, I saw women eating roasted corn they had cooked on little fires. The old Coptic church which we visited was said to have been the site where the Holy Family stayed when they left the murderous Herod and his soldiers who wanted to kill the Baby. We saw men and young boys carrying one hundred pound rocks to the site of a mosque which needed repair.

During our second day in Cairo, we visited the enormous empty pyramids decorated with well preserved paintings, and other stone buildings. I was amazed how well those huge stone giants have stood the test of time. It was exciting to mount a camel and have a short ride.

Our meals in Cairo provided a variety of foods. For breakfast, there were rolls, butter, jelly, cottage cheese, and coffee. The evening meal called dinner consisted of soup; a meat either of chicken, beef, or fish; a salad with tomatoes or cucumbers and watermelon. Once we had a fresh apple for dessert.

The lack of cleanliness made it necessary that we use the napkin to clean the dishes before we ate from them. There was no air conditioning so all the windows were open, letting in dust and insects.

The water was not safe to drink; we purchased bottled water all the while we were in Egypt.

I found the Middle East to be a man's world. Hotel personnel were all male. Men serve the meals, do the cleaning, and serve as chefs. The women have beautiful features; however, usually the women are covered from head to toe in black cloth.

My impressions of Egypt can be summed up a few words: poverty and multitudes of people. Cairo was like an ant hill, people constantly on the move on donkey carts, wagons with produce, camels, bicycles, motor cycles, cars, trucks, and buses. Since there was inadequate cooling system, it was scary to see carcasses of recently butchered animals hanging in the open air. The evening of August 3, we were treated to "Sights and Sounds," which showed three pyramids and the Sphinx as the stage for an historical review of the history of the Giza Pyramids. The event was very beautifully done and lasted for over an hour.

On August 4 we flew to Amman, Jordan, a beautiful hilly and clean city. I felt we were well-received and I compared it to the Promised Land that the Israelites entered. We were bused from Jordan to Madaba to view the famous Byzantine Church of St. George. This church has a mosaic floor map of Jerusalem as it existed in biblical times. In this church there is a statue of Our Lady of Perpetual Help with three hands, honoring a lady who was cured at a liturgy there.

On Mt. Nebo, we were told that it was from that point Moses viewed the Promised Land. There are beautiful mosaics in the church. Some Franciscans live in a monastery nearby. One mosque was off limits because Moslems were worshipping at that time. We drove past King Hussein's living palace, and also his working palace. After lunch we headed for Gerash, a beautifully preserved Greco-Roman city. Evacuations which began in 1920, revealed magnificent columns and stairways of the Temple Artemis. A Triumphal Arch was erected in the second century AD to welcome Emperor Hadrian. This city was built on the top of Byzantine, Greek, and Roman civilizations. Marks of the chariot wheels are still evident in the streets. Along the way I purchased in one of the many ever-present shops, a set of worry beads and a book of Jerash. Later in the evening we had dinner, and the liturgy was celebrated by the two priests in our group.

On August 6, we went on a rocky excursion to the Nabatean Capitol, the Rose City of Petra. There were many interesting sights along the way, including phosphate mines, large herds of sheep, Bedouins in their tents, very excellent highways, and rich soil which does not need the native phosphate. We were alerted about half way to Petra of the change in color of the soil, which resembled coal cinders. Our guide said that this was the place where God rained down fire and brimstone on the cities of Sodom and Gomorrah. After leaving this area, we saw that the soil and rocks looked white. As we drove along in the bus, we noticed the incline of the road. Eventually we mounted horses and went down the rocky canyon, finally coming to a Roman amphitheater, and having Mass celebrated with a group from Denver on this Feast of Transfiguration. After lunch, we made the four-hour drive back to Amman.

Israel was our destination on August 7. We traveled over the mountains of Gilead and the fertile valley of the Jordan, through two check points where we were warned not to show our passports, lest we not be allowed back into Jordan with an Israeli stamp on them. At customs we were given a thorough one-hour search, even having to take a picture of the ceiling to assure the agents our cameras were not guns. Finally we came to the Dead Sea and found it to be very salty and oily. We drove on to Qumran to see where the Dead Sea scrolls were found, and to see the remains of the monastery where the Essenes had lived.

At Jericho, we enjoyed a lunch of turkey, mashed potatoes, carrots, peas, and very sweet grapes. We drove on to Nazareth and had Mass in the Church of the Annunciation. We toured all the shrines, the carpenter shop, baptismal font, and all the icons in the upper church. After dinner back at the hotel, Father Jim and I went for a long walk around this important city.

The feast of St. Dominic, August 8, was a good day to go to Cana. On the way we passed the monastery where Charles de Facould lived for some time. After Nazareth, we went to the Mount of the Beatitudes, where Father Jim celebrated Mass on a cool patio. At a shop in Cana, I bought a bottle of wine which I shared with my brother and his wife at Christmas time.

We were eager to get to the Sea of Galilee where Jesus had multiplied the loaves, where Peter was named head of the church, and where Jesus cooked fish for the apostles' lunch. After our own lunch at the hotel, we took a taxi to the top of Tabor to the church where three priests live in a monastery and three nuns live in a convent. We noticed that two of the Italian nuns were milking a cow. From the top of Tabor, we could see for miles around.

August 9, we headed for Acre which is close to the Mediterranean Sea. This city is surrounded by walls built by the crusaders. We next went to Haifa, an industrial city, and the largest city in Israel.

The city has a few Arabs, but is mostly populated by Jews who had fled there from Germany. Farther north, Mass was celebrated on Mount Carmel.

A two- hour drive brought us to the great city of Jerusalem, where we stayed in Commodore Hotel in the beautiful Jewish University. Bedouins who live in black tents were guarding their sheep right outside the hotel. At Bethlehem, I drank my first Turkish coffee, which is very strong. We visited the manger where it is said that Jesus was born, and again we had the blessing of Mass. Some felt deep emotions at this holy spot and many tears were shed during the Mass in the Cave of the Shepherds. In the afternoon we visited the church of St. Catherine and the tomb of David, the site of the Last Supper, and the Church of Dormitian where it is said the Mary died. In the Church of Bethany we saw the tomb of Lazarus, and had Mass in the Basilica of the Agony in the Garden of Gethsemani. We also visited the church where Jesus was scourged; the Augustinians are in charge of this very small but important place in history.

August 13 saw our tour group headed for Athens via the Royal Jordanian. On August 14, we toured Athens, a city of about ten million people. We found that Greece had about 15,000 miles of coastline and it had many mountains; on top of many of these there were statues of the Greek gods. It was a thrill to visit Corinth, St. Paul's territory. From there we went to see the Parthenon, and to climb to its peak over rugged terrain. The climb down turned out to be dangerous for rain had fallen and the rocks were slick. We came to our hotel drenched.

On August 15 we boarded a ship to visit three islands along the Greek coastline, namely Agena, Poras, and Hydra. There were opportunities to do some shopping on these islands, and to watch people playing water polo and engage in swimming matches. A photographer ran among us taking our pictures, and a bit later came to sell us the copies. August 15 is a sacred day on the island of Poras where people are off the streets and not going to their jobs. At the end of the day, we returned to our ship and headed back to Athens. August 16 was a traveling day; we left Greece at 1:00 p.m. and landed in Rome at 3:00 p.m.

There was a special front row place arranged for our group to watch Pope John Paul II go by in his Popemobile, after he had arrived in a helicopter. During our wait to see him there was a shower; we had come prepared for that. What a rush of people clamoring to get nearer to His Holiness! In the afternoon we toured the Vatican Museum and the Sistine Chapel, the place where elections of the pope take place. We were privileged to pray at the tomb of Pope John XXIII. It seemed to me that St. Peter's is not a place designed for prayer, but to satisfy the curious eyes of tourists.

On the 18th of August, we attended Mass in St. Peter's at a shrine dedicated to St. Benedict. In our tour of the city, we saw many nuns in primitive habits. We visited the catacombs and these churches: St. Mary Major, St. John Lateran, and St. Maria Minerva, the church in which St. Catherine of Siena died and where her body is entombed. Other sights we saw in the Eternal City were the Fountain of Moses, the Four Fountains, the statue of St. Peter in chains by Michaelangelo, and the Trevi Fountain. I was eager to locate a congregation of Dominican Sisters whom some of my Sisters knew from their visits to Rome. Part of our group took a taxi on August 20, to their convent located at 142 V. Lanza. They mentioned Sisters Francesca, Betty Jean, and Louise whom they remembered with deep appreciation. Our congregation had helped these sisters when they had financial needs some years earlier. In gratitude, they continue to pray for the Great Bend Dominicans.

Even though this was an extra expense, we couldn't leave Europe without making a visit to Assisi, the home of St. Francis. We traveled over a highway built by the Romans about 200 BC. At the saint's tomb we celebrated Mass and then enjoyed a most delicious lunch, complete with good wine. We also visited the Church of St. Clare; there we found that ancient paintings had all been covered with paint because the former paintings had proved to be distractions to prayer. It seemed to me that all the great churches we visited were beautiful, but not as places of prayer, but as gigantic museums.

We returned to Rome that afternoon to begin our flight back to Amsterdam on August 21. We had a four- hour delay before we were ready to cross again the wide blue Atlantic, thus ending a most wondrous trip abroad.

Thanks, Mama, from the bottom of my heart for making this trip possible!

In Egypt on a camel on the way to see a pyramid

Ministry that Made my Heart Sing

"Our Lord and Saviour lifted up His voice
and said with incomparable majesty:
'Let all people know that grace comes after tribulation.
Without the cross they can find no road to climb to HEAVEN'."
(St. Rose of Lima)

Father Bob Schremmer, Pastor at St. John the Evangelist in Hoisington

With my name in God's hand, I was gently led away from little children in the classrooms, away from the world of library books, to a new and exciting time to share my gifts as a pastoral minister in St. John the Evangelist Parish in Hoisington, just ten miles from Great Bend. My focus in the parish according to the pastor, Father Bob Schremmer, was to minister for about twenty hours a week to widows and widowers, shut-ins, patients in hospitals, the lonely, the grieving, those yearning for a deeper spirituality, and those who just needed someone to listen to the stories of their lives.

I was blessed to very easily secure a house in which to live. This house belonged to Dick and Lil McGrath, and had recently been vacated by Sister Martina Stegman who was leaving Hoisington to minister in Hays.

My ministry began on the first of August, 1991, by visiting some shut-ins. I was given a list of those who needed my services, especially widows and widowers, about seventy in number, and I was off and running, making visits to get acquainted and finding out needs and interests. I spoke to the parish council, sharing with them what I had to offer, and receiving their full approval. When I visited with individuals to suggest forms of enrichment for their lives, I listened to many personal stories, stories of pain and joy. There were topics of interest suggested, schedules for teachings and listening periods were made, books and videos for study sessions were ordered, and interest was aroused by personal contacts and notices in the parish bulletin. Sunday readings were paramount to the schedule, and Morning Prayer was arranged for the period following daily Masses. Like all beginnings, attendance was sparse, but as the Spirit entered in and word spread around, attendance was greatly increased. Sharing times were rather stilted at the start, but as confidence was built, persons became more free to express their true feelings and the desires of their hearts.

My ministry spread to the Rehabilitation Center and to the hospital. The Eucharist was taken to Catholics, to shut-ins, and to the patients in the hospital. I attended the weekly Mass at the Rehabilitation Center and I often stayed to visit with those present.

In the interest of forming a Faith Community, I was assisted by Judy Linsner and we sought videos and books for sharing times. Parishioners were asked to sign up for a six-week session. These sessions were held in the afternoon and evenings once a week for six weeks, three times a year, namely in the fall, in the spring, and during Lent. Some of the videos we used were: *Gospel Attitudes, Life Crossroads, Cultural Blessings, Wrestling with Angels, Discovering Everyday Spirituality,* and *By Way of the Heart.* These books were used: *Vision 2000, Spirituality of Aging, Healing Wounded Emotions, Traits of a Healthy Spirituality, While You Were Gone,* and *Exploring the Sunday Readings.* During one semester we used videos to study the lives of the saints.

Besides these times of study and sharing, I became involved in the parish RCIA, offering support, and even serving as sponsor. I was part of the local ministerial association group and attended their meetings. There were birthdays to mark, celebrations at festive occasions, communal penance services, and instructions to give a former Catholic who returned to the church. A minister's wife, Jan Ogle, offered sessions for those who had lost a loved one; I joined the group and saw the healing of many grieving persons as they shared their losses.

There were community celebrations in which to be involved. Labor Day in 1992 was full of festivities; besides parades there was a cookout that Father Bob sponsored for priests and Sisters in the area. There was a float of a miniature St. John Church which was celebrating its Centennial. The bishop came to the parish on Labor Day to prolong the Centennial year and give First Eucharist to a class of about eighteen children. Another Centennial event was marked in November when the deceased members of the past year were remembered with special burning candles. On the 30th of November, 1992, our church was blessed with the ordination of Father David Flagor. At Christmas time, there was an open house for the parish and a tour of all the parish buildings. Some leaders were available to explain the vestments used for the liturgies. An outdoor Mass with two deacons from the parish present was a great event.

One of my greatest blessings during my first two-and-one-half years at St. John's was the presence of one of the diocese's finest priests, Father Bob Schremmer. He gave me the fullest support in all my endeavors, and I always knew that Father was a true pastor in every sense of the word. It was he who would be out shoveling snow long before Mass time. He would be in the sacristy early in order to prepare for the Mass, and he would be at the front door of the church greeting the congregation as people arrived. Father Bob was truly interested in everyone of his parishioners and they felt his love in all ways. His homilies spoke to all ages and offered everyone something to take home for the following week. He was a very neat and organized person; one had only to notice how well prepared he was for any parish meeting. He came with notes and schedule, and led meetings in a most efficient manner. Father Bob was very interested in how the sanctuary looked; everything was placed for the best possible effect.

When it came time to say goodbye to the most Christ-like priest I have ever met, there were tears in abundance. I learned that Father Bob was willing to make this change in order to help another priest who was having difficulties in ministry. Even though Father Bob loved St. John, he was open to making a change to help a brother priest. His unselfishness was a perfect example of the kind of priest he was. I told Father Bob as he was leaving that I felt like Christ had walked among us those past two and one half years. I grieved; the town grieved on that sad day January 19, 1994, when Father Schremmer departed to take up ministry at Sacred Heart Parish in Larned.

My only consolation at Father Bob's departure was the thought that others will now share his wonderful gifts.

God speed you, Father Bob on your way. Thanks for all the blessings you brought to St. John's.

Father Jack Maes Arrives at St. John the Evangelist Parish

January 20, 1994, saw the arrival of our new pastor, Father Jack Maes. I had not known Father, but he greeted me with a big hug. I found him very supportive of the ministries I already had in progress. At our staff meetings, Father made sure everyone had a chance to offer input.

In many ways Father Maes was a perfectionist, and he wanted everything in its proper place. At that time the church was suffering from old age, and there was a great need for renovation. The supporting beams need to be stabilized; there was need for new plaster and paint to cover all the walls. The pews needed to be sanded and upholstered, kneelers to be replaced, and new carpeting installed. The tabernacle was moved to the side of the sanctuary and two angel statues were placed there to support it. The choir loft was raised, and chairs replaced the pews. Glass front doors were installed. The Stations were reframed. The windows were given a protective covering which served in good stead when the tornado of 2001 struck the church, and spared all but two of the windows. All these changes gave St. John Church a very wonderful and clean appearance; it looked like a new church.

In an effort to lighten Father Maes' burden in his pastoral duties, the parish hired the recently trained liturgist, Sister Marie Zogleman ASC, to serve as liturgist. Her duties covered an entire page, ranging from liturgy ministry to serving on a variety of parish committees. Sister prepared the liturgies; decorated the altars; trained lectors, song leaders, servers, and ushers. Some thought that she considered every ministry hers, and some long-time personnel resigned. At times it seemed that her duties and mine overlapped, and this caused some friction. When the next pastor replaced Father Maes, Sister was not rehired.

Father Pascal Klein Arrives

November 9, 1999, was the date a new pastor, Father Pascal Klein, took over his duties in St. John Parish in Hoisington. Father Maes had been assigned to St. Andrew Parish in Wright. It was again a sad time to say goodbye, and I will always be grateful for the support I received while Father Maes was pastor.

There were a few changes evident but nothing major. Father Klein was rather a young priest and he believed that he could do all that Sister Marie had been doing, so he did not renew her contract. A Mass at the nursing home was scheduled for every Thursday. Since Father is bilingual, he could celebrate Mass in Spanish, German, Latin, and even in Italian. Those Thursday liturgies were followed by a social in the dining room, where much to the delight of the residents, Spanish and German foods were sometimes served.

I assisted Father in many ways, especially celebrating Communion Services at the Rehabilitation Center when needed. In this way, I kept my preaching skills in practice. During the week of collections for retired religious, Father asked me to speak on my religious vocation and my past ministries. I was aware that in the congregation I had several of my former students, even one who had become a pharmacist.

I had only gratitude to the three pastors and the good people of Hoisington, and a sense of accomplishment when I decided in May of 2001,to terminate my ministry in that parish. This new venture into pastoral ministry had been a step outside of my usual comfort zone, but with God's hand in mine, I felt a sense of security and knew God would be my strength and give me all the courage I would need. And God did just that and more!!!

Time to Say Goodbye

These are the two bulletin inserts at the time of my departure from Hoisington in May, 2002:

> *The time has come for me to say farewell. By the end of June, I will be leaving parish ministry. I treasure you people with whom I have worked the past eleven years. I am deeply grateful to have shared your friendship, care and generosity. You have truly been a blessing for me and my community.*
>
> *The time has come for me to at least partially retire from active ministry. I will continue to complete and animate our convent library after moving to Great Bend.*
>
> *If I have done anything to hurt anyone, I am truly sorry. Remain friends and partners of Christ who need your presence to enable God to keep pouring love into the hearts of humankind. Remain His companion, His beloved children, His joy! This is one way you can deepen your Christ life and thus help others.*
>
> *A good thing to do at retirement is to "Eat broccoli and do volunteer work."*
>
>   *Farewell and love you,*
>   *Sister Alvina*

Dear Parishioners,

The year 2002 has been a year of celebrating milestones. This past April, we have seen celebrated in our area a one year anniversary of the tornado, a parish history of 100 years at St. Catherine, a centennial of service from the Dominican Sisters of Immaculate Conception Convent in Great Bend.

Another milestone is the many years of Sr. Alvina Miller's faithful service to our parish community. Her ministry among us as a sacristan, a Eucharistic minister, a teacher, a sponsor, and a pastoral caregiver to the aged and shut-ins has endeared her to us. Her milestones of service have earned her the well deserved time for personal and communal enjoyment. We extend to her our deepest and warmest love and prayers for her ministry among us. The Staff and I, who have had the pleasure of working with her and learning much from her good counsel, shall miss her terribly. However, we know that she deserves time to revel in the light of the Lord and the companionship of her community and friends. As we have become accustomed by her presence among us, let our prayers be for Sr. Alvina to be accustomed to drawing from the joy of travel and community, the love of God and His beauty of creation. May God bless you and keep you, may He let His face shine upon you, all the days of your life.

Fr. Pascal

Sister Alvina Miller
Golden Jubilee

100th anniversary of the Hoisington parish.
Float with miniature church in the Labor Day parade

Celebrating 75th Jubilee and other Jubilees

St. Dominic as he traveled without his shoes, in the country

Our Family Crest . . .

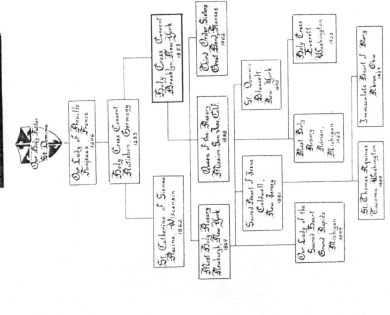

VERITAS

The upper left portion of the shield signifies the origin of the Congregation. The eagle is an emblem of Bavaria in which Ratisbon is located. The cross at the lower left signifies the Order of Preachers. The Marian symbol at the upper right indicates the title and patron of the Motherhouse. The M A is for Mary, and the crown honors her as Queen of the Rosary. At the lower right, the three gold roses of four petals each signify the twelve Congregations which grew from the parent Community at Ratisbon, Bavaria.

The motto, Veritas, Truth, is that of the Dominican Order.

Our family crest (tracing our linkage as a community)

They Broadened my Horizons
They Guided my Faltering Steps

"I am one of the women in their nineties and beyond
who continue to witness with stunning beauty
to the joy and fruitfulness of a life
totally given to God and to God's people."
(Sandra Schneiders)

Towering over all persons in this arena are my precious parents, my generous, loving Mama, and my tender-hearted Papa---my first teachers. Their deep religious faith and honorable ethic of hard work and play continue to be reflected in the values I hold today.

Father Dennis Mary McAuliffe OP offered many a challenge on my spiritual journey. He encouraged me to compose my personal Way of the Cross.

Sister Augustine Scheele (1896-1982), a School Sister of the Sisters of St. Francis in Alverno College in Milwaukee, was my star in my teaching career. She was described as a teacher with fire in her heart, a fire which made her competent, inspiring, and a great leader. As teacher and college president, she brought intensity to the field of religious education. She loved learning; she loved teaching and offered the highest ideals to her field. I have fond memories of a very interesting class she taught for teachers of religion. I caught some of her inspiration and began the process of encouraging children to learn by doing.

I will be ever grateful to my elementary teachers who set my feet on the path to learning reading, writing, and arithmetic. I recall

their names with fondness: Katie Billinger, Sophie Hammerschmidt, Barbara Sander, and Amelia Wasinger.

Another Sister Augustine (Haefele) was very influential in my early
religious life. I remember she met me and my family the day I entered and welcomed me as a postulant. As the director of my days
of postulancy and novitiate, she was always very kind and graciously accepted each of us on a daily basis. I call her a person with
a great sense of understanding .

Father Donald Heim was my spiritual director for five years. His
interest and concerns for my welfare were always a top priority.
He also shared his struggles and joys with me. This mutual communication made me feel that I was not the only one who had difficulties and joys. May God be very good to him as he shares the joys of
heaven. Father died July 24, 1994. May God be good to him.

Sister Renee Dreiling has been my spiritual director since the death
of my first director, Father Heim. I see her as a good listener, one
who is frank in letting me know just where I stand and what possible direction I should consider. Renee offers me challenges and
urges me to grow spiritually. Her smile lets me know that I am accepted by her as a person of worth. She doesn't leave me in the
dark and I find her to be always a most graceful, provocative, and
wise woman.

Sister Irene Hartman was so kind to keep encouraging me to get
my life story into book form. She told me it was too good a story to
store away in the archives of the convent. There it would never be
seen, except for a few people might read it. Thank you, Sister Irene
for your encouragement.

My Prayer Life in my Religious Community

LECTIO DIVINA
"Reading, you should seek...
MEDITATING you will find,
PRAYING you shall call
and
CONTEMPLATING, the door shall be opened to you."

In my early religious life, prayer was very simple. Our community prayers consisted of vocal prayer like the rosary, morning prayer, litanies, ejaculations, and the silent half-hour of meditation on Scripture. The community recited the Little Hours of Mary in Latin. To replace that Office, we now have the Divine Office or "Dominican Praise" with inclusive language. Today the Scriptures are now a basic, especially "Lectio Divina." This is a form of prayer which includes reading and pondering God's Word, and praying about that Word. Spiritual reading is very important; sometimes I spend two hours in spiritual reading. I must say that the rosary is not my favorite prayer. I prefer Lectio Divina and the Centering Prayer. I like the quiet time these two types of prayer offer, since loud repetition is not my favorite way of praying.

It is unfortunate that daily Mass is not always possible because of the shortage of priests available. I often question the fact that women are not allowed to be ordained. I personally know many women who are well educated and capable of giving thoughtful homilies.

I found it interesting that William R. Callahan compared contemplative prayer to crabgrass. He said that kind of grass grows everywhere. Its roots dig deep and bind the earth. It needs little care, is resistant to drought, wind, and sun. People can walk all over it and try to kill it. It will grow even through cracks in the sidewalks, and it can burst forth powerfully when conditions are favorable. I too need to be open to God's Spirit and allow my contemplative spirit to flourish in the best of conditions I can offer.

Centering Prayer

Centering prayer has its roots in the Hebrew Bible. In this type of prayer, the soul brings his/her sighing heart before God. Thomas Keating recommends that this prayer be done twice a day for twenty minutes. Why twenty minutes, why twice a day? Keating suggests that for most people it takes that much time to establish the necessary level of interior silence to move beyond superficial thoughts.

Here is the outline that I find suitable for my personality for the practice of centering prayer:

> I sit relaxed and quiet, and select a one syllable word. I try not to be in a reflective mode avoiding words, emotions, and thoughts that could interfere with the chosen word. When distractions come, I reject them and go back to the sacred word.
> I sit comfortably, with closed eyes, settling silently, and introducing the sacred word as a symbol of my consent to God's presence.
> Whenever I am aware of thoughts, I return gently to the sacred word.
> At the end of the twenty minutes, I remain in silence with eyes closed for a few minutes.

I am happy to say that this type of prayer leads to contemplation, according to Father Martinez OP. Since we live in such a busy world whose motto is hurry, hurry, hurry, I need this time of silence in order to act in a thoughtful way the rest of my day. I try to even read the newspaper in a serious way, and to make all my duties conform to a contemplative spirit.

It seems to me that centering prayer is very challenging and a great help to contemplation. I see contemplation as a deep penetration into the reality of things and of God Himself as a result of our union with Him in faith and charity. Contemplation to me means perceiving God and God's reflection in all things. Isn't it a resting in truth that is beyond word and image?

There have been at least three times in the recent past when I felt that I met God. The first time was during my thirty-day retreat in Sedalia, Colorado. It was such a powerful experience of God that it continued for weeks every time I prayed in the mode of centering prayer. The second time that I met God was one morning at Hoisington when I was engaged in centering prayer. The third time was when I had my left knee replaced on January 25, 2011, and was recovering in the infirmary. This experience was too sacred to commit to words. I believe that God never shows His face, but that moment was too powerful not to acknowledge. I take comfort in the words of 1 John 4:12 "No man has ever seen God; if we have love for one another, God abides in us and His love is perfected in us." I hold to the belief that God reveals Himself in faith as Isaiah wrote, "Truly you are a God who hides Himself, O God of Israel, the Savior." Again in Exodus, I believe what is written in Chapter 33, verse 20."You cannot see My face; for man shall not see Me and live." I anticipate my meeting God face to face in eternity.

Lectio Divina

In the practice of Lectio Divina, I try to masticate a Scripture passage and let its full flavor come forth. I find inspiration in what Blessed Jordan wrote to Blessed Diana, "Ruminate on, gaze on, absorb into yourself the whole mystery of Christ's love made effective in His death and resurrection." Again he wrote, "I want you, my daughter, to accustom yourself to dwell in these words." According to Father Timothy Radcliffe OP, "Sometimes the Lectio Divina of the Scriptures is quiet and peaceful. At other times one may argue with the text and wrestle with its meaning."

As a retired Sister in the Motherhouse, I have more time in which to learn to be at home in the Word of God. I am learning to take St. Dominic as an example of times when he meditated on the Scriptures and seemed to be talking directly to God. I make efforts to ensure that the silence and solitude do not isolate me because the purpose of regular observance is that the word of God may dwell abundantly in the convent. I read in the book of Wisdom, "God's all-powerful Word leaped forth when gentle silence enveloped all things."

I am proud of the founder of my Order, St. Dominic, who in the thirteenth century preached against the Albigensian heresy in southern France. In 1206, he gathered a band of converted women who were eager for truth amidst the dark confusion of their time. Their mission was to pray for the order of men whom he was so soon to establish. The mission of the nuns of the order continues to be to support the active ministries of the Dominican family. From Dominic's example, I learned what can be the outcome of prayer and study.

Today and every day I try to live the truth as Dominic exemplified. I feel personally responsible for continuing the vision that he had. I believe that God predestined the members of the Order to be persons whose lives cherish God's Word and deepen the quality of a contemplative life in today's world. I try to be free for God and live in community "with one mind and heart." Community life is sometimes difficult, but somehow it keeps me down to size as it elicits every virtue. I try to mirror the inner life of the Trinity in silence and solitude, thus feeding my efforts to contemplate.

I will present an example how I pray Lectio Divina, seeing it as a silent reflection on God's Word which I turn over and over in my heart and dwell in and gaze on the Word. For example, I choose Genesis 46:1-7 and 28-30. This chapter brings to Egypt the seventy members of the family of Jacob. I see God symbolically completing His plan, fulfilling His promise temporarily, but leaving the plan intact.

> My reflection includes these thoughts: Jacob's fears are calmed because he holds the promise of God that his descendants will be a great nation. I see him move again as Abraham once had to do in response to God's call. Jacob places the future of his family in God's hands.
> Secondly, I pray: Lord, come to my assistance especially in times when fears overcome me and when I am making a difficult decision. Teach me to trust. Teach me to develop a stronger relationship with You and to listen for Your Word rather than to do my own guessing.
> My action might be to consider setting aside a special time each day to grow in knowledge and appreciation for what the Lord has done and is doing for me.

This three-fold way of praying the Lectio Divina I learned from the New Revised Standard Version of the Bible.

I hold in faith that when I faithfully do the work of prayer, God will cut through the rock, the hardness of my heart, and the water can come forth. I look to my model, St. Dominic, and note that he had nine ways of prayer; in some ways my ways are like his.

> With body erect he would bow his head and heart humbly before Christ.
> He used to pray by throwing himself down on the ground, flat on his face and say, "Lord, be merciful to me a sinner."
> He used to take the discipline with an iron chain as a way of sorrowing for sin.
> Dominic would gaze on the crucifix, and genuflect again and again.
> One way of prayer was by standing erect.
> Dominic prayed with his hands and arms spread out like a cross.
> Dominic was often found stretching his whole body toward heaven in prayerful ecstasy.
> Sit quietly holding an open book, making the sign of the cross and reading (Lectio Divina).
> He would go aside from his companions, allowing them to go on ahead on a journey, while he lingered behind in prayer.
>
> Blessed Jordan said of Dominic that he believed Dominic had the singular gift of weeping for sinners.

The Way of the Cross

On one occasion when I was engaged in a reflective conversation with Father Dennis Mary McAufille, OP, he suggested that I compose my own set of the Stations of the Cross. This is the fruit of my efforts:

"All we like sheep have gone astray, every one into his own way, that is after his own lusts and delights; and the Lord has laid on Him the iniquity of us all."

"Arise, make haste, my love, my beautiful one and come. For winter is now past...the time of pruning is come."

Perfect charity seeketh not its own, spareth not itself if only God's honor be increased.

To love---to be loved and to return to the world and make Him loved (active and contemplative life).

It is characteristic of the cross that it comes to us "by chance."

"In all thy ways think on hIm, and he will direct thy steps."

"But one thing I do, forgetting the things that are behind and stretching forth myself to those that are before, I press toward the mark."

"If they do these things in the greenwood, what shall be done in the dry?" (If innocence is so severely punished, what will happen to me who have so often offended Him?)

"He that is mighty hath done great things to me." "He has shown me my littleness and incapabilities of all good." (St. Theresa)

"He must be sought for afar off." (Imitation) We must seek Him afar off, that is to say in lowliness, in nothingness, away from all that glitters, then shall we be truly poor in spirit.

"I to my Beloved, and my Beloved to me." Left to one's self, one suffers so much! Given over to God, one is so happy!

The dreadfulness of this death, my Jesus, is quite in keeping
with the hatefulness of sin.
"Come Lord Jesus!" If I truly possess You, my God, grant that I
may give You to others.
"If the seed dies, it will rise a hundredfold fruitful."

My heart sings a happy tune whenever I think of the precious gift
with which God blessed me, namely my prayerful Papa and Mama.
I will close this section of my prayer life with the English translation
of a German prayer that was special to Mama:

I thank You, dear Jesus, that You died for us.
Let not Your pain and suffering be lost on us.

The Gift of Tears

*"Tears are perhaps
the most rejuvenating and recreating water of all,
the evidence that love allowed the grace
to melt the ice at the center of my being.
Where there are tears, there is the Holy Spirit."*

"Jesus wept." There are many references to tears in Scripture.
John says in 11:35 "Jesus began to weep." Luke says, "Magdalen
wept on the feet of Jesus." Paul tells readers in Romans,
"Likewise, the Spirit helps us in our weakness, for we do not know
how to pray as we ought, but that very Spirit intercedes with sighs
too deep for words." When words fail us, God doesn't. Tears are
another language. In Genesis 50:17b to 18a, there is this section
about Joseph. "Now therefore please forgive the crime of the serv-
ants of the God of your father. Joseph wept when they spoke to
him. Then his brothers also wept. … ..Then Joseph threw himself
on his father's face and wept over him and kissed him." "God is
felt in places too deep for words," and one may break out in tears
which are an eloquence equal to the person's needs. Tears come
from the intensity of the light as the soul gazes on God. God's light
transforms.

Tears are sacred. Tears are not a sign of weakness but of the power the soul possesses. I believe that God sees tears as precious. I
find that my eyes sometimes fill with tears when I am touched by
something; tears are already in my heart and seek expression. At
times, my tears may come in solitude but I am not ashamed to
weep in public. My tears may signal a need I have, or they may signal I am experiencing the loving presence of God. Sometimes my
tears provide an insight into a new direction for my life. I believe I

have been gifted by God with tears. Tears can be the signal that points me away from myself and to another. Tears unite in me what is human with what is divine.

From the day I entered the convent, I was often in tears. At first, tears would flow and I was unable to discover the cause. I just cried, seemingly without reason. As I look back on those early days in Great Bend, I now believe that my tears were principally tears of joy. I had at last achieved the fulfillment of my lifelong dream, a dream to become a religious Sister.

I am grateful for the gift of tears because I see tears and contemplation as synonymous. They are both gifts of a deep encounter. My tears can begin to flow when I read a passage from Scripture, or when I sing or hear a hymn sung. I have to cease singing or reading and attend to my tear-filled eyes.

In the life of St. Dominic, I note that he too often wept. He seems to have been favored with a tenderness of heart which expressed itself in tears. When St. Dominic was sometimes praying for a solution to some doctrinal question, he would burst into tears. Blessed Jordan said of the holy man Dominic, "God gave Dominic the singular gift of weeping for sinners, the wretched and the afflicted, whose sufferings he felt within his compassionate heart."

God, I am grateful for the gift of tears.
May my tears show my compassion for all humankind.

Life after my 75th Jubilee

"The evening of a well-spent life
brings its lamps with it.
Growth in old age requires the curiosity of a five-year old,
the confidence of a teenager.
Old age is not when we stop growing.
It is exactly the time to grow in new ways.
It is the softening season when everything in us
is meant to achieve its sweetest, richest, most unique self."

Care of my Body

Life changes slowly. It was December of 2010 when my doctor suggested that I have a left knee replacement; I agreed. Why? In 1969 while I was stationed in Sapulpa, Oklahoma, I was in Tulsa for the Eucharistic Congress where I was eager to hear Bishop Charles Buswell speak. As I was taking a short cut, I fell on the cement walk and injured my knee. It was in 1971 that Dr. Biegler in Garden City removed the injured cartilage and the baker cyst.

Dr. RanJan Sachdev in Great Bend advised me in 2010 that I should have the knee parts replaced. He said that as a woman of ninety-three years, I was healthier that many who are a mere fifty. The very painful surgery was performed on January 25, 2011. My recovery accompanied by daily exercise took six weeks. I returned to an exercise regime called Curves where I had initially begun exercising in 2006.

Now my daily routine consists of early prayer, breakfast, exercise at Curves, and a couple of hours work in the library. Holy Mass or a Communion Service is usually at 11:15, followed by dinner. In the afternoon I take a nap, do some reading, some study, some prayer, and then join the community for Office and rosary at 5:00 p.m. I enjoy watching Dr. Oz and Wheel of Fortune.

As I look back on my days of active ministry, I note that many days were only WORK. Today I have the leisure to take time to be good to my body. I consider this care as a sacred trust. God gave me this healthy body, and I need to create a balance between prayer, work, and play in order to keep my good health. Research tells me that prayer and meditation can lower blood pressure and heart rate. My body is holy. When I take care of my body, I am also taking care of my spirit. I believe in having a rich prayer life. When my energy is high, I can hear God whispering to me. As I use the various exercise machines at Curves, my mind is cleared and my joints become more pliable. As a result I can pray and work better. There is another benefit that comes from my participation at Curves, namely the participants help others by being involved in gathering food, clothing, and funds to support the needy.

My Need for Solitude

In my days after my 75th jubilee, I have become more aware of the blessings that come from solitude. Today's world sees solitude as simplistic. I am aware and alert to my personal need for solitude. Psychology rates solitude as healthy and needed. As a religious, I have the special vocation to mirror Christ who often withdrew into solitude for prayer. I see solitude as essential to my getting away from the world's enticements. Jesus calls me to "come away by yourself to a lonely place." (Mk 6:31)

Even though I am not classed as a hermit, I still see the need for solitude. Both the Rule of St. Augustine and the life of St. Dominic beckon me to seek solitude and unity in community. I strive to live in harmony, intent on God in oneness of mind and heart; I strive to be united with my Sisters in community even in my solitude. I certainly don't need to search for an actual desert. I can taste the Word of God any place, but I actually find it easier to pray in solitude. In solitude, I strive to be open to being touched by the Word, to learn the depth of sin and weakness, even when this may be painful. Darkness can change to light in my times of prayer in solitude. My holy rule calls me to be willing to be in seclusion, unless duties, work, or obedience require my presence elsewhere. But I strongly believe that from the "interior cell of my heart," I need never depart.

I look to my model, St. Dominic. Blessed Jordan of the Romans said of St. Dominic, "No one was more a community man, nor more joyous." Dominic used to haunt the churches at night and devote himself to prayer in solitude. On his journeys he would allow his brethren to go on ahead, while he lingered behind, wrapped in prayer.

St. Dominic, teach me to be with my God in solitude.

The Velveteen Rabbit

As I move along in my retirement years, my mind often goes back to events of earlier times, such as a story that I remember. Long ago I read the story of *The Velveteen Rabbit* by Margery Williams. The story has made a great impression on me. In the classic story of a stuffed rabbit and the boy who received it as a Christmas gift, Margery Williams tells of the boy who received the stuffed rabbit but was snubbed by the other expensive and sophisticated toys as they flaunted their complexity and regarded themselves as real.

The rabbit asked if being real meant "having things that buzz inside you and a stick--out handle?" The Skin Horse replied, "Real isn't how you are made. It's a thing that happens to you. When a child loves you for a long, long time, not just to play with, but <u>really</u> loves you, then you become real."

"Does it hurt?" asked the rabbit. "Sometimes," said the Skin Horse, for he was always truthful. "When you are real, you don't mind being hurt." "Does it happen all at once, like being wound up bit by bit?" he asked. "It doesn't happen all at once," said the Skin Horse. "You become. It takes a long time. That is why it does not happen to people who break easily, or have sharp edges, or who have to be carefully kept. Generally, by the time you are real, most of your hair has been loved off and your eyes drop out and you get loose in your joints and very shabby. But these things don't matter at all, because once you are real, you can't be ugly except to people who don't understand."

I have lived seventy–six years as a professed religious Sister. Becoming real is a life-long process. If I persevere in the process of becoming real, I will have to work daily at cleansing my heart and actions of prejudice and discrimination, as well as from apathy that allows such injustice to go unchecked. I have to be truthful about my life. Becoming means that I admit my weakness and vulnerability, and offer these to God who will grace me with honesty about my sharp edges, my excessive sensitivity and fragility, and my desire to be carefully kept.

I must be willing to let my hair be loved off through dedicated service, and to accept that my joints may get loose. I may take on a shabby look when I attend more to the needs of others rather than to my own. Even though it hurts to become fully who I am called by God to be, it is important for me to make a new beginning. The process of becoming doesn't happen all at once. It takes time.

The process of becoming continues as life moves along. I have to be open to God at all times especially when God asks me to become a contemplative. This is a life-long process and it begins with letting go of all sin and imperfections. St. John of the Cross calls this time the active part of contemplation. When that part is nearly completed, God steps in and I have to become passive because God is taking over and takes away consolations and even the love of prayer that had previously been present. This is the "Dark night," according to St. John of the Cross. At such a time, I become powerless to meditate and it seems like all the joy of religious life vanishes. I believe that at such times God is preparing me for something better. If I remain submissive, stay rooted in faith, even though this may be a fearful time, I believe God is readying me for a new surprise.

My life has been good and there have been blessings too numerous to mention. However, not all my days have been blessed with roses, for I have had my share of hardships and difficulties. But I know that God keeps promises and along with the test, I will find a way out so that I may be able to endure and even grow through the hardships. I hold to the words of St. Francis de Sales:

> The everlasting God has in His wisdom foresaw from eternity the cross that He now presents to you as a gift from His inmost Heart. This cross He now sends you He has considered with His all-knowing eyes, understood with His divine mind, tested with His wise justice, warmed with His loving arms, and weighed with His own hands to see that it be not

one inch too large and not one ounce too heavy for you. He has blessed it with His holy Name, anointed it with His grace, perfumed it with His consolation, taken one last glance at you and your courage, and then sent it to you from heaven, a special greeting from God to you, an alms of the all-merciful love of God.

When my life comes to an end, I want to leave singing the words of Thompson:

Softly and tenderly Jesus is calling, calling for you and for me; see on the portals He's calling and watching, watching for you and for me.
Come home, come home, you who are weary come home. Earnestly, tenderly, Jesus is calling, calling for you to come home.
Why should we tarry when Jesus is pleading, pleading for you and for me? Why should we linger and heed not His mercies, mercies for you and for me?
O for the wonderful love He has promised, promised for you and for me! Though we have sinned, He has mercy and pardon, pardon for you and for me.

I offer two special quotes from my friend St. Paul, which have helped me in good times and in times that were not so good:

"Finally, we urge you and appeal to you in the Lord Jesus, to make more and more progress in the kind of life that you are meant to live, the life that God wants, as you learned from us and as you are already living." I Thessalonians 4:1-2

"Eye has not seen, ear has not heard, nor has it so much as dawned on us what God had prepared for those who love Him. Yet God has revealed this wisdom to us through the Holy Spirit." I Corinthians 2:9

In ending, I offer a quote from John of the Cross:

"Whither hast thou hidden Thyself, O my God, beloved, And left me to my sighing?"

MY LAST REQUEST AFTER I DIE :

God has blessed me with very good eyesight. Please take my CORNEAs. Give them to some very needy person.   Thank You.

ACKNOWLEDGMENTS

I feel so honored that my sister-in-law, Sister Alvina Miller, has graciously asked me to read her story.

I read the story that I titled, "Story of Life," with God as my main character, on my way to Texas to attend the passing of Sister's brother and my brother-in-law, Arthur Miller. The reflections I felt from Sister's stories and her faith journey helped prepare me for the days ahead in my life.

My faith life has matured, too, as I grow older and somehow, God is always a larger part of each and every day of my life. Sister's story has made me more aware of this need and gave me more insight how to proceed with each new day, seeing God present.

Thank you, Sister Alvina for who you are and continue to be to everyone you come in contact with. Your faith is a prayer of love, never ending and always shining brightly.

Gloria Miller

Journeying with Sister Alvina through the ups and downs in her life these last years has indeed been an honor and a privilege. Alvina is a woman of deep feelings and of deep faith. Her quest for knowledge leads her to read books of all kinds at a phenomenal rate! Often she would read and take notes on a book a week! These books would not be novels or small easy books, but books that challenge one to think and to look deeply at life, at injustice, at the mysteries of our faith and of our spiritual life.

(continues on next page)

Neither has Alvina's sharing about her own life been superficial. She delves into her thoughts, her feelings, her attitudes, and her actions. Always she does so with profound honesty, even when that honesty brings pain. Sometimes the pain brings exasperation, sonetimes tears, sometimes a struggle to understand. But always she uses it to grow as a person and to grow in her relationship with God. Her yearning to be in a deep love relationship with God is an intense one, spoken about often.

Sister Renee Dreiling

I share the same heritage of the Volga Germans as Sister Alvina Miller. We can share special foods, customs and stories of our Ancestors. I have come to know Sister Alvina a little better in the last few years. She is not only a friend and Sister in community but a wonderful mentor. I respect and learn from her wisdom gleaned from her life's experiences. Before reading her story I admired her quiet and gentle nature, the matter-of- fact way she approaches the ups and downs of her day to day struggles, and the acceptance and non judgmental attitude toward others.

After reading her story I can see how God had led her to become the person she is today. She inspires and shares with me what is helpful in my journey to God. Everyone including me has been blessed to have her in our lives.

Sister Imelda Schmidt

Reflections from Sister Charlotte Brungardt

Two things in particular have always impressed me about Sister Alvina Miller and these are quite evident in her life's story. First, I have been amazed at Sister Alvina's thirst for knowledge. She can devour a book, speak of it to others, and integrate that information with other things she has studied. I always appreciate it when she recommends a magazine article or book. Sisters who belong to the study group that she leads are thrilled to gather with her. She epitomizes the Dominican call to study.

Secondly, Sister Alvina has always put her gifts at the service of God's people. She made the transition from classroom teacher, to school librarian. A new need arose and she answered the call to hospital business office and to medical librarian. Later it was to parish minister, and now convent librarian. Sister Alvina has been faithful to the Dominican call to mission. May her memoirs help each person who reads them reflect upon his/her own faithfulness to God's call.

Additional Pages

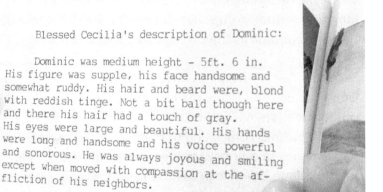

Blessed Cecilia's description of Dominic:

Dominic was medium height - 5ft. 6 in. His figure was supple, his face handsome and somewhat ruddy. His hair and beard were, blond with reddish tinge. Not a bit bald though here and there his hair had a touch of gray. His eyes were large and beautiful. His hands were long and handsome and his voice powerful and sonorous. He was always joyous and smiling except when moved with compassion at the affliction of his neighbors.

Have charity
one for another,
guard humility
and make your
treasure out of
voluntary poverty.

-St. Dominic's last will and testament

SISTER ALVINA MILLER
Was born on Sunday, February 17, 1918

The Year's Top Story

US celebrates Germany's surrender as World War ends.

News of the Month

All Broadway theaters closed to save coal.
New Jersey "anti-loafing" law requires all able-bodied men to work.
President authorizes takeover of property of enemy aliens.

People Who Share Your Birthday

1902	Marian Anderson Concert singer
1907	Marjorie Lawrence Australian opera
1908	Red Barber Baseball announcer
1936	Jimmy Brown Football player
1925	Hal Holbrook Actor
1844	Montgomery Ward Montgomery Ward stores

People Your Age

......Leonard Bernstein......
........Billy Graham.........
.........Ann Landers.........
......Abigail Van Buren......

Famous Firsts

Kelvinator refrigerator, Wonder
Bread, Bayer aspirin marketed ... US
issued first airmail stamp and began
airmail delivery ... Rinso first
granulated laundry soap ...
Hydrofoil invented ... Broadmoor
Hotel in Colorado ... BELIEVE IT OR
NOT published in newspaper by Ripley

Fun Facts & More

PRESIDENT   Woodrow Wilson
VICE PRESIDENT   Thomas Riley Marshall

And the Winner Is...

Best Movie	Polly of the Circus
Best Actor	Vernon Steele
Best Actress	Mae Marsh
Newspaper	Stars & Stripes for Armed Forces
Song	Swanee by George Gershwin
World Series	Boston Red Sox over Chicago Cubs
Boxing (Heavyweight)	Jess Willard
Kentucky Derby	Exterminator - W. Knapp up

Tunes of the Times

K-K-K-Katy ... I'm Always Chasing Rainbows ...
Rock-a-Bye Your Baby ... Till We Meet Again
... Dear Little Boy of Mine ... After You've
Gone ... Beautiful Ohio ... A Good Man Is Hard
to Find ... Hinky Dinky Parlay Voo ... Mickey

Life in the U.S.A. — Then & Now

	1918	1988
Population	103,208,000	245,900,000
3 Br. Home	$3,325	$78,843
Avg. Income	$1,106	$29,896
New Ford	$525	$10,323
Gas, 1 gal.	$.25	$.99
Bread, 1 lb.	$.10	$.72
Milk, 1 gal.	$.54	$2.02

GARDEN OF ALLAH painted by Maxfield Parish as cover of tin candy box ...
Raggedy Ann doll introduced to promote Raggedy Ann stories by John Gruelle, who
first created the doll and stories for ill daughter ... TILL WE MEET AGAIN top
sheet music best seller ... Vaudeville acts were big, toured US in Kieth or
Orpheum circuit ... Sgt. Alvin York awarded Congressional Medal of Honor in WWI

OCCUPATIONAL EXPERIENCE

YEAR	PLACE	INSTITUTION	POSITION
1937-1939	Odin, Ks	Holy Family School	Grades 1-2
1939-1940	Wichita	Sacred Heart College	Student
1940-1941	St. LEO	St. Leo School	Grades 1-2
1941-1946	Garden City	St. Mary's	Grades 1-4
1946-1947	Seward	St. Francis Xavier	Grades 1-4
1947-1949	Great Bend	St. Rose School	Grade 3
1949-1851	Willowdale	St. Peter Achool	Grades 3-4
1951-1952	Garden City	St. Mary School	Grade 1
1952-1953	Garden City	St. Catherine Hosp	Business Office
1953-1955	Garden City	St. Mary School	Grade 1
1955-1958	Sharon	St Bonfice School	Grades 1,2 *Principal*
1958-1960	Great Bend	St. Rose School	Grade 1
1960-1961	Pueblo, Colo.	Asumption School	Grade 3
1961-1962	Schulte	St. Peter School	Grades 3,4
1962-1964	Wichita	Magdalen School	Grade 6
1964-1966	Sharon	St. Boniface School	Grades 3,4,5 *Principal*
1965-1968	LaCrosse	St. Michael School	Grades 3-4 *Principal*
1968-1971	Sapulpa, Okla	Sacred Heart School	Grades 5-6 *Principal*
1971-1972	St. Louis, Mo.	Marillac College	Sabbatical
1972-1974	Wichita	Magdalen School	Librarian
1974-1975	Garden City	St. Dominic School	Librarian
1975-1976	Garden City	St. Dominic School	Libratian
		St. Mary School	Librarian
1976-1077	Garden City	St. Dominic	Librarian
		St. Mary School	Librarian
1977-1978	Garden City	St. Mary School	Librarian
1978-1979	Garden City	St. Mary School	Librarian
1979-1980	Garden City	St. Mary School	Librarian
		St. Catherine Hosp	Librarian
1981-1982	Garden City	St. Catherine Hosp	Librarian
1982-1983 Feb	Garden City	St. Catherine Hosp	Librarian Microfilm
1983-1984	Great Bend	CKMC	Librarian
1983 July	Traveled to 5 countries		
1984-1985	Great Bend	CKMC	Librarian
1985-1991	Great Bend	CKMC	Librarian
1991-Aug 2001	Hoisington	St. John Evangelist	Pastoral Minister
2001 May	Great Bend	Convent	Librarian
2008	Great Bend	Convent	Librarian
2013	" "	"	"

St. Mary's Convent, Great Bend, Kans.

THE ORIGINAL CONVENT—the Central Normal College—when the Sisters from Brooklyn first came to Kansas.

THE RATISBON CLOISTER—the roots of the Sisters of St. Dominic in Great Bend.

A BANNER expresses several stages in the growth of the Great Bend Community.

Remembrances of my Parents

Papa

- Strong belief in justice
- Listening to her read German Stories
- His closeness to me
- Great care for family
- Often saw him cry
- Sense of humor
- Very conservative with money
- Very Tender Hearted

Mama

- Held authority in family
- Cleanliness
- Her discipline in raising us—often very strict
- Her pride in finally having a son
- Her knowledge—in spite not having attended school
- Making due with Little
- Stories she told about our ancestory
- Her generosity in feeding and helping others

"Viewed as a challenge, retirement is not the end of one's professional life. It is just a change of jobs. The work years are far from over, the work ahead is just of a different kind.

There is much to be done.

The time has come to empty oneself of bitterness, of envy, of selfishness, of a drivenness that may have let one overlook the feelings of others.

It is time for the gentler side of oneself to flower. Perhaps there is yet time to mend some fences, to right some wrongs, to restablish some valued human connections.

Of course, it is quite possible at this juncture in life to make a quite different choice: to withdraw from others, to retreat comfortably within oneself, and to let the rest of the world go by.

Worse yet, one could become bitter and self-pitying, wasting precious time in bemoaning the lost past.

Either of these options would result in a self-defeating kind of existence. If, for self-protection, we have woven a cocoon about ourselves, it is now time to let the butterfly emerge. It is in freeing the self, in emptying the self, that we can be open to receive the life-expanding gifts of friendship, peace, happiness, new ideas, a deeper kind of living. Shrouded in a cocoon, we would not grow."

This is one part of a reading I came across in the book by Maria Reilly, S.P. Now That I Am Old, Meditations on the Meaning of Life.

I so often feel that my retirement time is so full of new adventures, so filled with inner peace, so challenging in many respects, and so filled with an interior joy that never happened before. Perhaps I was always so busy with so many duties that I was so exhausted and didn't take the time to feel the joys of life.

THE BUTTERFLY HAS EMERGED

YOU DOMINICAN WOMAN are called
TO CONTEMPLATE

the Presence of GOD everywhere —
in the WORD of Scripture,
in the Wisdom of Creation,
in beauty, truth, and justice,
in sacramental daily living,
in our sisters and brothers,
    the eagle, the violet, the child,
in the most forgotten and neglected,
in the events of our times,
in the church,
    the communion of faithful ones.
YOU ARE CALLED

to live and to give
the fruit of this Contemplation

REMEMBERING THE GOOD IN MY LIFE

My parents always encouraged my vocation to Religious Life.

That we finally had a brother after 12 years of praying.

That I was accepted into the Community in Great Bend.

That Sister Aloysia believed in having all the sisters educated up to a Masters Degree, and a few PHD

The times in the classroom I spent with many little children and prepared them for their First communion.

The privilege of making a 30 day retreat in Sedalia, Colorado.

That my mother gave the the privilege of traveling to five different countries namely Cairo, Egypt, Amman, Jordan, Greece, Italy, Israel.

The great blessing of becoming a parish Minister in Hoisington at St. John Evangelist.

That I had good relations with all three pastors in Hoisinton while serving there as Pastoral Minister.

The wonderful things I have learned from senior members whose life experiences I have shared.

That I have very good eyesight expecially after having cataracts removed. Now 20/20 vision except for reading.

To have had Fr. Donald Heim as my spiritual director. Also that he invited me to come to Philadelphia to visit him after he re- tired. He also showed me many of the Historical places in Philadelphia and Washington D.C. including the shrine of the Immaculate Conception.

That I have had good health almost all of my life.

PEOPLE WHO STRONGLY SHAPED AND INFLUENCED MY LIFE

Father Norman our Pastor at St. Severin
Church at the time of my entrance into
the Dominican Community at Great Bend, Ks.

My parents, of course who always gave and
encouraged me in whatever I needed to do.

Sister Augustine, my Novice Mistress when
I entered the community.

Sister Aloysia, who really taught us about
Religious Life even though she was very
strict in her beliefs.

Fr. Jim Sheehan, our chaplain for a number of
years and who asked me to tour with him and
sixteen other members to five countries.

Fr. Donald Heim, who was my spiritual director
for many years he was here in Kansas. It was
difficult for me when he left to go to Philadelphia
to retire because of illness. While there he invited
me to come and visit.

Fr. Pascal Klein, was the Pastor in Hoisington
while I was stationed there. Father is a very
good Confessor.

Fr. Bob Schremmer, who also was in Hoisington
while I was stationed there during my time in
Hoisington. He was the one who encouraged me to
use my talents in helping Senior members of the
parish.

TURNING POINTS IN MY LIFE

My entrance into Dominican community in Great Bend.

Making my first vows in the Great Bend Dominican Community

Retiring from teaching after thirty two years, 1971

My thrity day Ignatian Retreat in Sedalia, Colorado, 1983

Having a very good spiritual director for many years,
    Father Donald Heim

Being hired as Pastoral Minister by Fr. Bob Schremmer in
    the Hoisington parish.

Having another good pastor in the Hoisington St. John
    Evangelist parish, Fr. Pascal Klein.

Working with the senior members of the Hoisington parish.

Loss of papa in death, 1971

Loss of mama in death, 1989

The 2005 July retreat in preparation for my 70th Jubilee

My Jubilee day celebrated in July 23, 2005 with the
    Community, 70th

Being able to obtain the BOOK SYSTEMS library system which
    enables us to order catalogue and have all the book
    on the computer, and many other advantages.

Being semi-retired and able to take time for my spiritual
    life. Just about three hours for daily work. Age 83

At times like these there is always a letting go after each
and before another change. Often very difficult, but most of
the time a great blessing. In the void there was always a meaning

The three weeks travel to five different countries namely, Cairo, Egypt,
    Amman, Jordan, Israel, Greece and Rome, 1983
The week spent with Father Heim in Philadelphia. Father Heim was my Spiritual
Director for many years. In Philadelphia we spent three days visiting W.D.C
the national Shrine of the Immaculate conception, the Capitol and many other
historical places.

Jenifer Jones
Sister Alvina
Maria Miller
Gloria Miller

Jenifer Jones
Sister Alvina
Maria Miller
Gloria Miller

Group at the
Dinner Table

Jeff Miller
(took pictures)

Gilbert Urban
Mary Ann Urban
Sister Alvina
Maria Miller
Gloria Miller
Cecil Miller

Mary Ann Urban
Sister Alvina
Gilbert Urban

Cecil Miller
Sister Alvina

GOLDEN JUBILEE

Sr. Ronald Weiss
1303 E. 18th Street
Hays, Kansas 67601

July 07, 2005

It is a time of celebration!!!

I am writing this letter to share with you a most important celebration in my sister's life. Sr. Ronald left to join the religious community of the Sisters of St. Agnes in Fond du Lac, Wisconsin when I was just two years old. She had just turned 14. Back then, trains still were the main means of transportation across the miles. Imagine, if you will, the spirit of a young girl leaving her family behind to join a community of nuns halfway across the country!! "Back then" that took a great deal of courage and conviction, not to include reciting a rosary or two.

The first three years of a nun's life (as a **Candidate**), back then, were spent in high school, while living as a member of the community. Those years were about learning to understand what a life devoted to Christ was about, sacrificing the traditional family life, learning the essence of perfect obedience, poverty and chastity. These early formative years were dedicated to provide the structure, the time of work and prayer, and the ground work for a particular vocation within the community. In 1953, Sr. Ronald was "invested" and became known as a **"Novice"**. It was a period of commitment dedicated to prayer and reflection (the novitate) designed to prepare her for the next stage of her religious life. Her **Profession** formally and publicly proclaimed her vows before God, her community, and her family. This is the time in her life we celebrate now. She subsequently renewed those vows and in 1961 she made those **Final Vows** as a bride of Christ.

It isn't easy to describe what a nun's life is all about. Within our biological family, Sr. Ronald is the oldest and I am the youngest with an eleven year difference in our ages, yet we have the closest sibling relationship. I believe that is because we both know what part a physical distance from the rest of the family/relatives plays. I have had the opportunity to experience an upfront look into her life as well as that of the community. For that opportunity I am eternally grateful and it is one that I wish everyone could have in their life. Through the experience I have known peace, unconditional love, unending prayers and thoughtfulness, and dedication to knowing Christ's way of life. Through the years, rules for her community involvement have changed. Years ago home visits were limited, a time when relatives "back home" were growing up and dating and getting married and having families of their own. It became a time when separation really took hold because family events were missed, not in spirit, but in dedication to a calling, a religious vocation.

My big sister, Sr. Ronald, now resides in Hays with a "new" vocation, so to speak. She is still a nun, still an integral part of the Sisters of St. Agnes. When our "Mom" initially could no longer care for herself, Sr. Ronald asked her Order's permission to move to Hays and care for our parents. It was a "different" sort of ministry and Sr. Ronald received the blessing of the congregation in her quest. While she resides with Dad, she is affiliated with the nuns who are also in the Hays area. Her responsibilities are far reaching and too numerous for me to keep up with.

I write this letter to each of you because while our family is not celebrating with a formal affair, I want to bring this joyous time to everyone's attention. It is a milestone in the life of the person I most admire in my life. I have included her address above.

Respectfully,

Dominican
Sisters of Peace

Sisters and Associates
in Mission

January 30, 2015

Alvina Miller, OP
Great Bend Motherhouse
3600 Broadway Ave
Great Bend, KS 67530-3692

Dear Sister Alvina,

Congratulations on your 80th Jubilee! Thank you for your faithfulness to our Dominican mission for 80 years. I ask God for special blessings on you as you anticipate this anniversary celebration.

According to our policy, the congregational celebration of our Golden Jubilarians will take place during the Chapter in April. It is our hope that the 60, 65, 70, 75, and 80 year Jubilarians will celebrate at Motherhouses, Health Care Centers, and at Rosary Manor. The Mission Group Coordinators will plan for these celebrations, and you will receive information about the dates and times.

Blessings on your Jubilee year! May it be a year of special grace and peace for you.

In the Peace of Christ,

A. Therese

Therese Leckert, OP
for the Leadership Team

2320 Airport Drive | Columbus, OH 43219 | **www.oppeace.org**

voice: 614.416.1900 | *fax:* 614.252.7435 | *toll free:* 1.855.OPPEACE (1.855.677.3223)

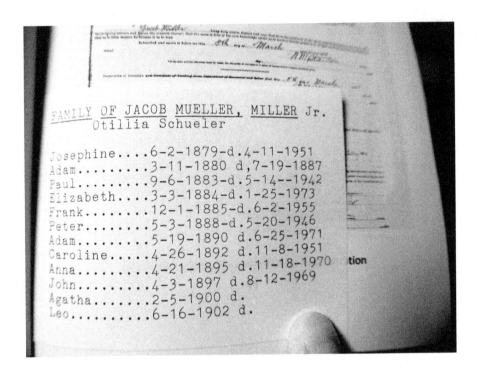

FAMILY OF JACOB MUELLER, MILLER Jr.
    Otillia Schueler

```
Josephine....6-2-1879-d.4-11-1951
Adam.........3-11-1880 d,7-19-1887
Paul.........9-6-1883-d.5-14--1942
Elizabeth....3-3-1884-d.1-25-1973
Frank........12-1-1885-d.6-2-1955
Peter........5-3-1888-d.5-20-1946
Adam.........5-19-1890 d.6-25-1971
Caroline.....4-26-1892 d.11-8-1951
Anna.........4-21-1895 d.11-18-1970  tion
John.........4-3-1897 d.8-12-1969
Agatha.......2-5-1900 d.
Leo..........6-16-1902 d.
```

Note: For a facsimile of Jacob Mueller Miller's Petition for Naturalization paper (the background page shown in the photograph above), see page 19.

LIFE BEGINS AT 80

I have good news for you. The first 80 years are the hardest. The second 80 are a succession of birthday parties.

Once you reach 80, everyone wants to carry your baggage and help you up the steps. If you forget your name or anybody else's name, or an appointment or your own telephone number, or promise to be three places at the same time, or can't remember something, you need only explain that you are 80.

Being 80 is a lot better than being 70. At 70 people are mad at you for everything. At 80 you have a perfect excuse no matter what you do. If you act foolishly, it's your second childhood. Everybody is looking for symptoms of softening of the brain.

Being 70 is no fun at all. At that age they expect you "to have it all together" and complain about your arthritis (they used to call it lumbago) and you ask everybody to stop mumbling because you can't understand them. (Actually, your hearing is about 50 percent gone.)

If you survive until you are 80, everybody is surprised that you are still alive. They treat you with respect just for having lived so long. Actually, they seem surprised that you can walk and talk sensibly.

So please, folks, try to make it to 80. It's the best time of life. People forgive you for anything. If you ask me, life begins at 80.

SISTER ALVINA MILLER
LIBRARIAN

106

Made in the USA
Coppell, TX
08 April 2023

15407829R00105